The AI Toolkit

Essential Methods, Practices, and Tools for Effective Machine Learning

Greyson Chesterfield

COPYRIGHT

DISCLAIMER

The information provided in this book is for general informational purposes only. All content in this book reflects the author's views and is based on their research, knowledge, and experiences. The author and publisher make no representations or warranties of any kind concerning the completeness, accuracy, reliability, suitability, or availability of the information contained herein.

This book is not intended to be a substitute for professional advice, diagnosis, or treatment. Readers should seek professional advice for any specific concerns or conditions. The author and publisher disclaim any liability or responsibility for any direct, indirect, incidental, or consequential loss or damage arising from the use of the information contained in this book.

Contents

Introduction

Artificial Intelligence (AI) and Machine Learning (ML) have become defining technologies of our era, reshaping industries, revolutionizing problem-solving, and sparking an unprecedented wave of innovation. From chatbots that simulate human conversations to algorithms that diagnose diseases with higher accuracy than seasoned doctors, AI has transcended the realms of science fiction to firmly plant itself in everyday life. The possibilities seem limitless, but for many, the journey into AI remains a daunting prospect, fraught with complexities and technical jargon. This book, *The AI Toolkit: Essential Methods, Practices, and Tools for Effective Machine Learning*, is designed to break down these barriers, providing a comprehensive yet accessible guide to understanding, building, and deploying AI and ML systems.

Whether you're a curious beginner eager to demystify these technologies, an intermediate learner striving to sharpen your skills, or a professional aiming to enhance your expertise, this book has been crafted with you in mind. Combining theory with practical application, the *AI Toolkit* offers a roadmap to mastering essential concepts, tools, and techniques while equipping you with actionable insights and hands-on projects to apply what you learn. This introduction sets the stage for what's ahead, exploring why AI and ML matter, how they work, and the principles that make them successful.

The Rise of AI: Why It Matters

In 1956, at the Dartmouth Summer Research Project, the term "Artificial Intelligence" was first coined, marking the birth of an idea that machines could mimic human intelligence. Decades later, AI has grown from speculative theory to practical reality, powered by advancements in computing, availability of vast datasets, and groundbreaking research. Today, AI influences nearly every aspect of modern life.

AI systems recommend what we should watch, buy, or read. They power self-driving cars, enable personalized medicine, optimize supply chains, and even create art. This rapid adoption is underpinned by Machine Learning, a subset of AI that empowers machines to learn from data and improve their performance without being explicitly programmed.

The surge in AI adoption is driven by three key factors:

1. **Exponential Growth in Data**: The digital era has generated an ocean of data, a crucial ingredient for training AI systems. With every click, swipe, or transaction, we produce information that AI can analyze and learn from.

2. **Advancements in Hardware**: High-performance GPUs, TPUs, and other specialized hardware have made it possible to train complex ML models faster and more efficiently than ever before.

3. **Open Source Tools and Frameworks**: Tools like TensorFlow, PyTorch, and Scikit-learn have democratized AI, lowering the barriers to entry and empowering individuals and organizations to build AI solutions.

The implications of AI are profound. It promises to solve problems once considered unsolvable, uncover hidden patterns in data, and augment human creativity. But with great power comes great responsibility. Ethical concerns, biases in algorithms, and fears of job displacement are critical challenges that must be addressed as we move forward.

Understanding the Basics: How AI and ML Work

At its core, AI refers to systems that exhibit traits we associate with human intelligence, such as reasoning, learning, and decision-making. Machine Learning, as a discipline within AI, focuses specifically on enabling machines to learn from data and improve their performance without being explicitly programmed.

How Machines Learn

Imagine teaching a child to recognize animals. You show the child pictures of dogs and cats, pointing out the unique characteristics of each. Over time, the child learns to identify dogs and cats even in unfamiliar images. Similarly, ML algorithms learn patterns from labeled datasets (supervised learning) or find hidden structures in data without explicit labels (unsupervised learning).

The three primary types of ML are:

1. **Supervised Learning**: The algorithm learns from labeled data. For example, predicting house prices based on historical data of houses (size, location, etc.) and their prices.

2. **Unsupervised Learning**: The algorithm finds patterns in unlabeled data. For instance,

clustering customers based on purchasing behavior without predefined categories.

3. **Reinforcement Learning**: The algorithm learns through trial and error by interacting with its environment and receiving rewards or penalties. This approach powers applications like game-playing AI and robotics.

The Role of Data

Data is the lifeblood of AI. Without data, algorithms are like cars without fuel. However, the quality, quantity, and diversity of data significantly impact the performance of ML models. One of the critical steps in any ML project is data preprocessing, which involves cleaning, transforming, and preparing data for analysis.

The Importance of Models

Models are the mathematical representations that AI systems use to make predictions or decisions. For instance, a model trained to recognize spam emails might analyze words, phrases, and metadata to determine the likelihood of an email being spam. Choosing the right model for a specific task is both an art and a science, requiring a deep understanding of the problem at hand and the capabilities of various algorithms.

Why This Book?

With a proliferation of AI resources available online, what sets this book apart? The *AI Toolkit* bridges the gap between theory and practice, presenting complex topics in a way that is approachable yet thorough. Our focus is not just on teaching you *what* to do, but also *why* it matters and *how* to do it effectively.

Key features of this book include:

- **Comprehensive Coverage**: From foundational concepts to advanced techniques, we leave no stone unturned.

- **Real-World Applications**: Each chapter highlights practical use cases, demonstrating how AI is applied across various industries.

- **Hands-On Projects**: Gain practical experience with step-by-step tutorials and projects that reinforce your learning.

- **Focus on Tools**: Learn to use essential tools and frameworks like Python, TensorFlow, Scikit-learn, and cloud-based AI platforms.

- **Addressing Challenges**: Explore ethical considerations, biases, and deployment challenges to build responsible and robust AI systems.

Who Is This Book For?

AI is no longer the domain of academics or large tech companies. It is a tool that individuals from diverse backgrounds—developers, analysts, entrepreneurs, and hobbyists—can leverage to solve problems and innovate. This book is designed for:

- **Beginners**: Learn the fundamentals of AI and ML without prior expertise.

- **Intermediate Learners**: Deepen your understanding with advanced topics and practical examples.

- **Professionals**: Stay ahead of the curve with insights into cutting-edge tools and techniques.

- **Hobbyists**: Explore AI as a creative and intellectual pursuit, applying it to personal projects.

Whether you're building your first predictive model or deploying AI systems at scale, this book will guide you through the process step-by-step.

What Lies Ahead

The *AI Toolkit* is organized to take you on a journey, starting with the basics and gradually progressing to advanced topics. The chapters are structured to build on each other, ensuring a logical progression of ideas:

- **Learn the Fundamentals**: Understand the essential building blocks of AI and ML, including data, algorithms, and tools.

- **Master Techniques**: Delve into supervised and unsupervised learning, deep learning, NLP, computer vision, and more.

- **Apply Your Knowledge**: Work on hands-on projects that simulate real-world scenarios.

- **Prepare for the Future**: Gain insights into emerging trends and ethical considerations in AI.

Each chapter combines theory with practice, featuring clear explanations, code examples, and illustrations to make even the most complex concepts accessible.

The Promise of AI

The future of AI is as exciting as it is uncertain. As these technologies continue to evolve, they will unlock new opportunities, solve pressing global challenges, and redefine how we live and work. But this future is not predetermined; it depends on how we choose to shape it.

The purpose of this book is not just to teach you how to use AI but to empower you to create, innovate, and contribute to this rapidly evolving field. With the right knowledge and tools, you can harness the power of AI to make a meaningful impact, whether it's in your career, your community, or the world at large.

So, let's dive in. The world of AI awaits.

Chapter 1: Introduction to AI and Machine Learning

Artificial Intelligence (AI) and Machine Learning (ML) are no longer just buzzwords; they are transformative forces reshaping our world. From self-driving cars to personalized shopping recommendations, these technologies are deeply embedded in our daily lives. Yet, for many, the concepts remain elusive or shrouded in mystique. What exactly are AI and ML? How did they evolve, and why are they so significant today? In this chapter, we will explore these questions, setting a strong foundation for your journey into this dynamic and rapidly evolving field.

What is Artificial Intelligence (AI) and Machine Learning (ML)?

At its core, **Artificial Intelligence** refers to the simulation of human intelligence in machines that are programmed to think, reason, and make decisions. It is a broad field encompassing various sub-disciplines, including Machine Learning, Natural Language Processing (NLP), robotics, and more. The ultimate goal of AI is to create systems that can perform tasks typically requiring human intelligence, such as understanding language, recognizing images, or solving complex problems.

Machine Learning, a subset of AI, focuses specifically on enabling machines to learn from data. Instead of being explicitly programmed with specific rules, ML systems use algorithms to identify patterns, adapt to new information, and improve their performance over time. For example, instead of coding a program to recognize cats in images based on predefined rules, ML allows a computer to analyze thousands of labeled images and "learn" to identify cats on its own.

The relationship between AI and ML can be visualized as follows:

- **AI**: The broader concept of creating intelligent systems.

- **ML**: A specific approach within AI, emphasizing learning from data.

To understand this better, consider AI as a field analogous to medicine. Just as medicine encompasses various specializations like cardiology and neurology, AI includes ML, NLP, robotics, and more.

Historical Perspective and Evolution of the Field

The journey of AI and ML spans decades, marked by breakthroughs, setbacks, and exponential progress in recent years.

The Early Days: The Birth of AI (1950s-1970s)

The origins of AI can be traced back to the mid-20th century when pioneers like Alan Turing and John McCarthy began exploring whether machines could emulate human intelligence. In 1950, Turing introduced the concept of the **Turing Test**, a benchmark for determining whether a machine could exhibit behavior indistinguishable from a human.

In 1956, the term "Artificial Intelligence" was coined at the Dartmouth Summer Research Project. This event is considered the birth of AI as a field of study. Early successes included:

- Development of simple problem-solving programs like the Logic Theorist (1955) and the General Problem Solver (1957).

- Creation of rule-based systems that used predefined instructions to simulate intelligence.

However, the lack of computational power and data hindered progress, leading to periods of stagnation known as the "AI Winters."

The Emergence of Machine Learning (1980s-1990s)

In the 1980s, **Machine Learning** emerged as a distinct approach within AI, focusing on statistical methods rather than rule-based programming. Key developments during this period included:

- **Neural Networks**: Inspired by the structure of the human brain, neural networks became a foundational concept for ML. Although early models were simplistic, they paved the way for modern deep learning.

- **Decision Trees and Bayesian Models**: These statistical approaches allowed machines to make predictions and classify data more effectively.

The increased availability of data and better algorithms began to revive interest in AI.

The Big Data Revolution and the Rise of Deep Learning (2000s-Present)

The 21st century marked a turning point for AI and ML. Several factors contributed to this resurgence:

1. **Explosion of Data**: The proliferation of the internet, smartphones, and sensors generated an unprecedented amount of data, fueling ML systems.

2. **Advancements in Computing Power**: The rise of GPUs and distributed computing enabled the training of complex models at scale.

3. **Deep Learning**: A subset of ML, deep learning uses multi-layered neural networks to achieve remarkable accuracy in tasks like image recognition and language processing.

Milestones in this era include:

- The success of IBM's Watson in winning *Jeopardy!* (2011).

- Google DeepMind's AlphaGo defeating world champion Go players (2016).

- The rise of large-scale language models like OpenAI's GPT series.

Today, AI is ubiquitous, driving innovations across industries and becoming a cornerstone of technological progress.

Key Differences Between AI, ML, and Data Science

While the terms **Artificial Intelligence**, **Machine Learning**, and **Data Science** are often used interchangeably, they represent distinct domains with overlapping goals. Understanding their differences is crucial for anyone navigating this field.

Artificial Intelligence (AI)

- **Definition**: AI is the overarching field aimed at creating intelligent systems capable of mimicking human cognitive functions.

- **Scope**: Broad, including robotics, expert systems, ML, NLP, and more.

- **Applications**: Self-driving cars, voice assistants, and game-playing bots.

Machine Learning (ML)

- **Definition**: A subset of AI focused on building systems that learn from data to improve over time.

- **Scope**: Includes supervised, unsupervised, and reinforcement learning.

- **Applications**: Spam filters, recommendation systems, and fraud detection.

Data Science

- **Definition**: A multidisciplinary field that extracts insights from data using statistical, computational, and domain-specific methods.

- **Scope**: Broader than AI and ML, encompassing data analysis, visualization, and engineering.

- **Applications**: Business analytics, market research, and healthcare diagnostics.

In simple terms, Data Science focuses on extracting knowledge from data, Machine Learning emphasizes learning patterns within data, and AI aims to use this knowledge to create intelligent systems.

Why Now? The Current State of AI and Its Impact

The question "Why now?" often arises when discussing the meteoric rise of AI and ML in the last decade. Several factors have converged to make this the perfect era for AI to flourish.

1. Data Abundance

The digital age has generated vast amounts of data, often referred to as the "new oil." Social media, IoT devices, e-commerce platforms, and sensors produce data at an unprecedented scale. This abundance provides the raw material ML models need to learn and improve.

2. Computational Advancements

Modern AI requires immense computational power to process data and train models. The availability of high-performance GPUs, cloud computing platforms, and distributed processing frameworks has made this feasible. Companies like NVIDIA and Amazon Web Services (AWS) have played pivotal roles in democratizing access to computational resources.

3. Open Source Ecosystem

The rise of open-source tools like TensorFlow, PyTorch, and Scikit-learn has dramatically lowered the entry barrier for AI development. These frameworks provide pre-built algorithms and extensive documentation, enabling even beginners to experiment with AI.

4. Economic Incentives

Businesses have recognized the economic potential of AI. From automating mundane tasks to providing personalized customer experiences, AI offers tangible benefits that translate into higher efficiency and profitability.

Impact on Industries and Society

The influence of AI extends across nearly every sector:

- **Healthcare**: AI is revolutionizing diagnostics, drug discovery, and patient care. Systems like IBM's Watson are being used to recommend cancer treatments.

- **Finance**: Fraud detection, algorithmic trading, and credit scoring are powered by ML.

- **Retail**: Personalized recommendations, inventory management, and customer insights are transforming e-commerce.

- **Transportation**: Autonomous vehicles and logistics optimization are reshaping the way goods and people move.

- **Education**: Adaptive learning platforms like Khan Academy tailor educational content to individual students.

However, the societal impact of AI is a double-edged sword. While it holds the promise of solving pressing global challenges, it also raises concerns about job displacement, data privacy, and ethical implications.

AI and ML are not just technologies; they are enablers of a smarter, more connected future. From their conceptual origins to their present-day dominance, these fields have evolved rapidly, driven by data, computational advancements, and human ingenuity. As we stand on the cusp of further breakthroughs, understanding AI and ML is no longer optional—it is essential for navigating the modern world.

This chapter has provided a comprehensive introduction to AI and ML, exploring their definitions, historical evolution, key differences, and current impact. As you move forward, remember that AI is not just about algorithms or data; it is about solving problems, enhancing lives, and shaping the future. Let this be the beginning of an exciting and transformative journey into the world of Artificial Intelligence and Machine Learning.

Chapter 2: Getting Started with Machine Learning

Machine Learning (ML) is a powerful subfield of artificial intelligence that enables systems to learn patterns from data and make predictions or decisions without being explicitly programmed. Its applications range from recommending products to automating complex industrial processes, and its adoption continues to grow across industries. However, starting with ML can feel daunting due to its breadth and perceived complexity. This chapter provides a clear roadmap to get started with ML, outlining the workflow from data to deployment, debunking common myths, and introducing popular ML applications.

The ML Workflow: From Data to Deployment

Machine learning projects follow a structured workflow to move from problem definition to delivering actionable insights or predictions. Each step is crucial to the project's success, and understanding this process will help beginners approach ML systematically.

---

1. Define the Problem

The first step is identifying the problem you want to solve and determining whether ML is the right approach. ML is ideal for problems where patterns can be learned from data, such as:

- Predicting numerical values (regression).
- Classifying items into categories (classification).
- Grouping similar data points (clustering).

Example:

A retail business might use ML to predict customer churn based on purchasing history and engagement metrics.

---

2. Collect and Prepare Data

Data Collection

The quality and quantity of your data are critical for building effective ML models. Sources can include:

- Databases (e.g., sales records, transaction logs).

- APIs (e.g., weather or social media data).

- Sensors (e.g., IoT devices for temperature or motion).

Data Cleaning

Raw data often contains errors, duplicates, or missing values. Cleaning involves:

- Removing irrelevant or redundant features.

- Filling or dropping missing values.

- Addressing outliers.

Feature Engineering

Feature engineering transforms raw data into meaningful input features that improve model performance. Techniques include:

- Scaling numerical features to a uniform range.

- Encoding categorical variables into numerical formats (e.g., one-hot encoding).

- Creating new features from existing ones (e.g., calculating ratios or time differences).

3. Split the Data

Divide your dataset into:

- **Training Set**: Used to train the ML model.

- **Validation Set**: Used to tune hyperparameters and avoid overfitting.

- **Test Set**: Used to evaluate the model's final performance on unseen data.

Example:

Split the dataset into 70% training, 15% validation, and 15% testing.

---

4. Choose an ML Algorithm

Selecting the right algorithm depends on the problem type and dataset. Common algorithms include:

- **Linear Regression**: Predicting continuous values.

- **Logistic Regression**: Binary classification tasks.

- **Decision Trees**: Versatile for both classification and regression.

- **K-Means Clustering**: Grouping data points into clusters.

- **Neural Networks**: Complex tasks like image or speech recognition.

---

5. Train the Model

Training involves feeding the training data to the chosen algorithm, allowing it to learn the relationships between input features and the target variable. During this process:

- The model adjusts its parameters to minimize errors.

- Iterative optimization methods like gradient descent are used.

---

6. Evaluate the Model

Assess the model's performance on the validation or test set using evaluation metrics such as:

- **Accuracy**: Percentage of correctly predicted outcomes (classification).

- **Mean Squared Error (MSE)**: Average squared difference between predicted and actual values (regression).

- **Precision and Recall**: Measure the model's ability to handle imbalanced datasets.

7. Tune the Model

Improve the model's performance by:

- Adjusting hyperparameters (e.g., learning rate, number of layers).

- Using techniques like cross-validation to ensure generalizability.

8. Deploy the Model

Once satisfied with the model's performance, deploy it to a production environment for real-world use. Common deployment options include:

- **APIs**: Host the model as a RESTful API using Flask, FastAPI, or Django.

- **Cloud Platforms**: Deploy on services like AWS SageMaker, Google AI Platform, or Azure ML.

- **Embedded Systems**: Integrate the model into mobile apps, IoT devices, or edge devices.

9. Monitor and Maintain

ML models require ongoing monitoring to ensure they perform well in production. Changes in data distributions (data drift) or model degradation necessitate retraining or updating the model.

Common Myths and Misconceptions About ML

While ML is a powerful tool, its complexity has given rise to many myths that can discourage beginners or lead to unrealistic expectations.

---

1. "ML is Only for Experts"

Reality

While advanced ML projects require deep expertise, many entry-level tasks are approachable for beginners with basic programming and math skills. Tools like Scikit-learn and TensorFlow provide pre-built libraries that simplify the process.

---

2. "ML Always Requires Huge Datasets"

Reality

While more data often leads to better models, small datasets can also yield valuable insights when combined with techniques like data augmentation or transfer learning.

---

3. "ML Models Are Perfect"

Reality

No ML model is perfect. Models are probabilistic and make errors, especially when trained on biased or incomplete data. Proper evaluation and iterative improvement are essential.

---

4. "ML Can Solve Any Problem"

Reality

ML is not a silver bullet. It's unsuitable for problems without patterns or where rules-based systems are sufficient.

---

5. "AI Will Replace All Jobs"

Reality

AI automates repetitive tasks but also creates new opportunities by augmenting human capabilities. It enables workers to focus on creative, strategic, and complex problem-solving tasks.

---

6. "ML is Too Expensive"

Reality

Cloud platforms and open-source tools have made ML accessible to individuals and small businesses. Pay-as-you-go models reduce upfront costs.

Overview of Popular ML Applications

ML is already transforming industries and everyday life. Here are some of the most impactful applications across domains.

---

1. Healthcare

Diagnostics and Imaging

AI-powered systems analyze medical images to detect conditions like cancer, fractures, or cardiovascular diseases.

- **Example**: Deep learning models identify abnormalities in X-rays with high accuracy.

Personalized Medicine

ML tailors treatment plans based on a patient's genetic makeup, lifestyle, and medical history.

- **Example**: AI algorithms recommend optimal cancer therapies based on genomic data.

Predictive Analytics

Hospitals use ML to predict patient admissions, optimize resource allocation, and prevent readmissions.

---

2. Finance

Fraud Detection

ML identifies unusual patterns in transaction data to flag potential fraud.

- **Example**: Credit card companies use anomaly detection models to prevent unauthorized transactions.

Algorithmic Trading

ML models analyze market data to execute trades at optimal times, maximizing profits.

Credit Scoring

ML evaluates creditworthiness by analyzing diverse data points, enabling fairer lending decisions.

3. Retail and E-Commerce

Recommendation Systems

ML suggests products based on user behavior, purchase history, and preferences.

- **Example**: Amazon's "Customers who bought this also bought" feature.

Inventory Optimization

Retailers use ML to forecast demand and optimize stock levels.

Customer Sentiment Analysis

Analyzing customer reviews and feedback to improve products and services.

4. Transportation

Autonomous Vehicles

ML enables self-driving cars to perceive their environment, make decisions, and navigate safely.

- **Example**: Tesla's Autopilot uses computer vision and reinforcement learning.

Traffic Management

Cities deploy ML to optimize traffic flow and reduce congestion.

5. Natural Language Processing (NLP)

Chatbots and Virtual Assistants

AI-driven systems like Siri, Alexa, and Google Assistant use NLP to understand and respond to user queries.

Machine Translation

ML models translate text or speech between languages in real time.

- **Example**: Google Translate's neural machine translation.

Sentiment Analysis

NLP analyzes social media posts or reviews to gauge public opinion.

---

6. Manufacturing

Predictive Maintenance

ML predicts equipment failures by analyzing sensor data, reducing downtime and costs.

Quality Control

Computer vision systems inspect products for defects on assembly lines.

---

7. Agriculture

Crop Monitoring

Drones equipped with ML algorithms analyze soil and crop health.

Yield Prediction

ML predicts crop yields based on weather data, soil quality, and planting techniques.

---

8. Education

Adaptive Learning

AI systems customize educational content based on a student's strengths and weaknesses.

- **Example**: Duolingo uses ML to adapt language lessons.

Automated Grading

ML automates grading of assignments, freeing up educators for other tasks.

Getting started with machine learning can seem overwhelming, but understanding the ML workflow provides a clear roadmap for success. From defining the problem and preparing data to training and deploying models, each step builds towards creating impactful solutions. By debunking common myths, we can demystify ML and make it accessible to anyone willing to learn. The potential applications of ML are vast, spanning industries and domains, and the skills you gain today will prepare you for an AI-driven future. With the right mindset and tools, anyone can embark on the exciting journey of machine learning.

Chapter 3:
Understanding Data

Data is the foundation upon which the entire field of Machine Learning (ML) is built. It is the raw material that feeds algorithms, enabling them to learn patterns, make predictions, and deliver insights. Without data, even the most sophisticated algorithms would remain powerless. In this chapter, we will delve into the critical role data plays in Machine Learning, explore its various types, and discuss the essential processes of ensuring data quality and preprocessing. By the end of this chapter, you'll have a solid understanding of why data is the cornerstone of ML and how to prepare it effectively for model training.

The Importance of Data in Machine Learning

Imagine building a house without bricks, mortar, or cement—it's an impossible task. Similarly, in Machine Learning, data is the building block that empowers models to function effectively. High-quality data ensures that models perform accurately, while poor data can render them unreliable, biased, or even useless.

Why Data is Crucial

1. **Learning Patterns**: Machine Learning algorithms rely on data to identify patterns. For example, a recommendation system learns from past customer behaviors to predict what products a user might like. Without data, these patterns cannot emerge.

2. **Generalization**: Models are designed to generalize from training data to unseen scenarios. This ability depends on the quality and diversity of the training data. Poor data leads to models that overfit (memorize instead of learning) or fail to adapt to new inputs.

3. **Decision-Making**: In applications such as fraud detection, medical diagnostics, or autonomous driving, accurate decisions hinge on reliable data. Faulty or incomplete data could lead to catastrophic outcomes.

4. **Model Validation**: Data is not just for training; it's also vital for testing and validating models. A good validation dataset ensures that the model performs well across different scenarios.

Types of Data in Machine Learning

Data in ML comes in various forms, and understanding these types is essential for selecting appropriate algorithms and preprocessing techniques. Broadly, data can be categorized into three types: **structured, unstructured**, and **semi-structured**.

1. Structured Data

Structured data is organized, easily searchable, and stored in predefined formats such as tables or spreadsheets. It is highly organized and typically involves rows (instances) and columns (features).

- **Examples**:
    - Customer data: Name, age, gender, and purchase history
    - Financial records: Revenue, expenses, and profit margins
    - Sensor readings: Temperature, humidity, and pressure

- **Characteristics**:
    - Highly organized and easy to analyze using SQL or similar tools

- Best suited for supervised learning algorithms like regression or classification

2. Unstructured Data

Unstructured data lacks a predefined format, making it harder to analyze directly. It is often text-heavy, image-based, or audio-visual in nature.

- **Examples:**
  - Text: Emails, social media posts, and chat logs
  - Images: Photos, medical scans, and satellite images
  - Audio/Video: Voice recordings, music, and videos

- **Characteristics:**
  - Requires advanced processing techniques such as Natural Language Processing (NLP) or computer vision
  - Often larger in volume compared to structured data

3. Semi-Structured Data

Semi-structured data lies between structured and unstructured data. It has a loose organizational structure but does not conform to strict table-like formats.

- **Examples**:
    - JSON and XML files
    - Web logs
    - IoT data streams
- **Characteristics**:
    - Flexible and versatile
    - Requires specialized tools like NoSQL databases for storage and retrieval

---

Data Quality and Why It Matters

The phrase "garbage in, garbage out" is particularly true in ML. Poor-quality data can lead to biased models, inaccurate predictions, and loss of trust in AI systems. Ensuring data quality is therefore a critical step in any ML project.

Characteristics of High-Quality Data

1. **Accuracy**: The data must be correct and free of errors. For instance, a customer's age cannot be negative.

2. **Completeness**: Missing data can skew results. If 30% of records lack critical fields like income or location, the model may underperform.

3. **Consistency**: Data should be consistent across all sources. For example, a user's email address in one database must match the same user's email in another.

4. **Relevance**: The data must be pertinent to the problem at hand. Irrelevant data increases noise and reduces model performance.

5. **Timeliness**: Outdated data may not reflect current trends, leading to poor predictions.

Common Data Quality Issues

1. **Missing Values**: Fields with missing entries can disrupt analysis and model training.

2. **Outliers**: Extreme values can distort statistical measures and mislead algorithms.

3. **Duplicate Records**: Repeated entries inflate data volume without adding new information.

4. **Noise**: Irrelevant or incorrect information that obscures true patterns.

Impact of Poor Data Quality

- Biased models that favor certain outcomes

- Increased training time due to noisy or irrelevant data

- Misleading insights that can harm decision-making

Data Preprocessing Essentials

Data preprocessing is the critical process of transforming raw data into a format suitable for analysis and model training. It involves several steps, each designed to enhance the quality and usability of the data.

1. Data Cleaning

Cleaning is the first step in preprocessing, addressing issues such as missing values, duplicate records, and outliers.

- **Handling Missing Values:**

    - Replace missing entries with the mean, median, or mode (imputation).

- o Use algorithms that can handle missing data directly (e.g., certain tree-based models).

- **Removing Outliers**:

  - o Use statistical methods like z-scores or interquartile ranges (IQR).

  - o Visualize data with boxplots to identify anomalies.

- **Eliminating Duplicates**:

  - o Remove duplicate rows to ensure accurate statistics.

2. Data Transformation

Raw data is often not in a format suitable for ML algorithms. Transformation involves converting data into a usable form.

- **Normalization and Scaling**:

  - o Scale numerical features to a standard range, such as 0-1, to ensure no single feature dominates the model.

  - o Common techniques include Min-Max scaling and Standardization.

- **Encoding Categorical Variables**:

- o Convert categories into numerical values using one-hot encoding or label encoding.

- o Example: Convert "Red," "Green," and "Blue" into [1, 0, 0], [0, 1, 0], and [0, 0, 1].

- **Feature Engineering**:

  - o Create new features or modify existing ones to improve model performance. For example, combine "Date of Birth" and "Today's Date" to create a new feature: "Age."

3. Data Integration

In many cases, data comes from multiple sources. Integration combines datasets into a unified structure.

- **Example**: Combine sales data from different regional offices to create a comprehensive dataset.

4. Data Reduction

Large datasets can be computationally expensive to process. Data reduction simplifies the dataset while retaining critical information.

- **Dimensionality Reduction**: Use techniques like Principal Component Analysis (PCA) to reduce the number of features.

- **Sampling**: Select a representative subset of the data when processing the entire dataset is infeasible.

Data is the lifeblood of Machine Learning, and its importance cannot be overstated. Understanding the different types of data—structured, unstructured, and semi-structured—is crucial for selecting appropriate techniques and tools. Equally important is ensuring data quality and performing meticulous preprocessing to prepare the data for analysis.

By mastering these concepts, you'll be equipped to handle one of the most critical aspects of any ML project: working with data effectively. Remember, the success of an ML model often hinges more on the quality of the data than the complexity of the algorithm. With clean, well-prepared data, you'll be well on your way to building powerful, accurate, and reliable ML systems.

Chapter 4: Essential Mathematics for Machine Learning

Machine learning (ML) is often perceived as a highly technical field, and mathematics forms the foundation of its principles, algorithms, and applications. While it is possible to implement machine learning models using modern frameworks without deep mathematical knowledge, understanding the core mathematical concepts provides valuable insights into how these models work, why they behave as they do, and how to improve them. This chapter explores three critical areas of mathematics for ML: linear algebra and its applications, probability and statistics as the foundation for decision-making, and gradient descent with optimization techniques. These topics empower you to move from being a practitioner to someone who truly understands the inner workings of ML systems.

1. Linear Algebra and Its Applications in Machine Learning

Linear algebra is at the heart of many machine learning algorithms. It provides the tools to work with high-dimensional data, model relationships between variables, and perform efficient computations. From representing datasets to optimizing models, linear algebra is indispensable.

1.1 Basics of Linear Algebra

Vectors

- A **vector** is a one-dimensional array of numbers representing a point in space or a set of features.

- **Example**: A vector x=[3,5,7]\mathbf{x} = [3, 5, 7]x=[3,5,7] could represent a data point with three features: height, weight, and age.

Matrices

- A **matrix** is a two-dimensional array of numbers, often used to store datasets or transform data.

- **Example**: A dataset of 100 samples with 5 features can be represented as a 100×5100 \times 5100×5 matrix.

Operations

1. **Addition and Subtraction**: Performed element-wise.

2. **Scalar Multiplication**: Multiply each element of a vector or matrix by a scalar.

3. **Dot Product**: Measures the similarity between two vectors.

1.2 Applications of Linear Algebra in Machine Learning

1.2.1 Representing Data

- **Feature Vectors**: Each data point is represented as a vector, and a dataset becomes a matrix.

- **Example**: In image recognition, a grayscale image of size 28×2828 \times 2828×28 pixels is flattened into a vector of 784 features.

1.2.2 Linear Transformations

- Matrices are used to perform transformations such as scaling, rotation, or projection of data.

- **Example**: Principal Component Analysis (PCA) uses eigenvectors and eigenvalues to reduce data dimensionality.

1.2.3 Training Models

- In linear regression, the goal is to solve the equation y=Xw\mathbf{y} = \mathbf{X}\mathbf{w}y=Xw, where y\mathbf{y}y is the target vector, X\mathbf{X}X is the input matrix, and w\mathbf{w}w is the weight vector.

- Finding the optimal w\mathbf{w}w requires solving a system of linear equations.

1.2.4 Neural Networks

- Neural networks rely heavily on matrix multiplications to compute activations and propagate errors during backpropagation.

Key Concepts

- **Norms**: Measure the length or magnitude of a vector.

  - **L2 Norm**: Used in regularization to prevent overfitting.

- **Singular Value Decomposition (SVD)**: Decomposes a matrix into simpler matrices for applications like recommendation systems.

---

2. Probability and Statistics: Foundations for Decision-Making

Probability and statistics are essential for machine learning because they provide the framework for making decisions under uncertainty. Models rely on probabilistic reasoning to make predictions, classify data, and measure confidence.

2.1 Basics of Probability

Probability Theory

- Probability quantifies the likelihood of an event.

- **Key Formula:**
  P(A)=Number of favorable outcomesTotal number of outcomesP(A) = \frac{\text{Number of favorable outcomes}}{\text{Total number of outcomes}}P(A)=Total number of outcomesNumber of favorable outcomes.

Random Variables

- A random variable represents outcomes from a probabilistic experiment, often used to model features in datasets.

Distributions

- **Probability Distribution**: Describes the likelihood of different outcomes.

- Common distributions in ML:

    o **Bernoulli Distribution**: Binary outcomes (e.g., success/failure).

    o **Gaussian (Normal) Distribution**: Continuous data with a bell-shaped curve.

    o **Poisson Distribution**: Counts of events over a fixed interval (e.g., customer arrivals).

2.2 Applications in Machine Learning

2.2.1 Bayesian Inference

- Machine learning models often incorporate prior knowledge using Bayes' theorem: P(A|B)=P(B|A)P(A)P(B)P(A|B) = \frac{P(B|A)P(A)}{P(B)}P(A|B)=P(B)P(B|A)P(A)

- **Example**: Naive Bayes classifier uses Bayesian inference to predict the probability of a class given input features.

2.2.2 Hypothesis Testing

- Used to determine if observed data aligns with a hypothesis.

- **Example**: Testing whether adding a new feature improves model accuracy.

2.2.3 Probabilistic Models

- Algorithms like Hidden Markov Models (HMMs) and Gaussian Mixture Models (GMMs) rely on probabilistic reasoning.

2.2.4 Uncertainty in Predictions

- Probabilistic models estimate confidence intervals for predictions.

- **Example**: In weather forecasting, a model might predict a 70% chance of rain.

Key Concepts

- **Conditional Probability**: Probability of an event given that another event has occurred.

- **Expectation and Variance**:

  o **Expectation**: Average outcome of a random variable.

  o **Variance**: Measures the spread of data.

- **Entropy:** Quantifies uncertainty in a distribution, used in decision trees and information theory.

---

3. Gradient Descent and Optimization Basics

Optimization is at the core of machine learning, enabling models to learn from data by minimizing error or maximizing likelihood. Gradient descent is one of the most widely used optimization techniques in ML.

3.1 What is Gradient Descent?

Gradient descent is an iterative optimization algorithm that minimizes a loss function by adjusting model parameters in the direction of steepest descent (negative gradient).

Mathematical Foundation

The gradient of a function represents its slope or rate of change. For a loss function $L(\mathbf{w})$, the gradient is given by $\nabla L(\mathbf{w})$.

3.2 Types of Gradient Descent

1. **Batch Gradient Descent**

   - Updates parameters using the entire dataset.

   - **Advantage**: Stable convergence.

   - **Disadvantage**: Computationally expensive for large datasets.

2. **Stochastic Gradient Descent (SGD)**

   - Updates parameters for each data point.

   - **Advantage**: Faster updates.

   - **Disadvantage**: High variance in updates.

3. **Mini-Batch Gradient Descent**

   - Combines batch and stochastic approaches by using small subsets of data.

3.3 Applications of Gradient Descent

3.3.1 Training Neural Networks

- Gradient descent updates weights during backpropagation by minimizing a loss function, such as cross-entropy or mean squared error.

3.3.2 Linear and Logistic Regression

- Gradient descent finds the optimal weights to minimize the error in predictions.

3.4 Challenges and Solutions

Challenges

1. **Local Minima**: The algorithm may get stuck in a suboptimal solution.

2. **Slow Convergence**: Learning rates that are too small can make optimization slow.

3. **Overfitting**: Fitting too closely to training data leads to poor generalization.

Solutions

1. **Learning Rate Schedulers**: Adjust the learning rate dynamically.

2. **Momentum**: Adds a fraction of the previous gradient to smooth updates.

3. **Regularization**: Penalizes overly complex models (e.g., L1 or L2 regularization).

3.5 Optimization Variants

1. **Adam Optimizer**

   - Combines momentum and adaptive learning rates.

   - Widely used for deep learning tasks.

2. **RMSProp**

   - Scales gradients based on recent magnitudes, improving convergence in non-stationary environments.

3. **Newton's Method**

   - Uses second-order derivatives for faster convergence but is computationally intensive.

Mathematics forms the backbone of machine learning, enabling us to build, optimize, and interpret models. Linear algebra provides the tools to represent and manipulate data efficiently, while probability and statistics help us model uncertainty and make data-driven decisions. Gradient descent and optimization techniques allow us to train models and refine their performance iteratively. By mastering these essential mathematical concepts, you gain a deeper understanding of machine learning, empowering you to tackle complex problems and innovate in this dynamic field. With this foundation, you are well-equipped to dive into the practical aspects of implementing ML algorithms and advancing your skills further.

Chapter 5: Supervised Learning Fundamentals

Supervised learning is a foundational concept in machine learning (ML), enabling systems to learn from labeled data to make predictions or decisions. By training models on input-output pairs, supervised learning creates algorithms that can generalize to unseen data. It's widely used in applications ranging from predicting house prices to detecting spam emails. In this chapter, we'll delve into the fundamentals of supervised learning, explore popular algorithms like linear regression, decision trees, and support vector machines (SVMs), and examine practical examples and case studies that illustrate its real-world applications.

Understanding Labels and Outputs

At the heart of supervised learning lies the concept of labeled data, which serves as the foundation for model training.

1. What Are Labels and Outputs?

Labels

- Labels are the target values or outputs associated with each data point in a dataset. They represent the correct answer the model aims to predict.

- Example:

    o In a housing dataset, the label might be the price of a house.

    o In a spam detection task, the label could be "spam" or "not spam."

Outputs

- Outputs are the predictions generated by the supervised learning model. The goal is to align these outputs with the true labels during training.

---

2. Types of Supervised Learning Problems

2.1 Regression

- Regression problems involve predicting continuous numerical values.

- Example: Forecasting a company's quarterly revenue.

2.2 Classification

- Classification problems involve assigning inputs to discrete categories or classes.

- Example: Categorizing emails as spam or not spam.

---

3. Training and Testing

1. **Training Phase**: The model learns the relationship between inputs (features) and outputs (labels) by minimizing error.

2. **Testing Phase**: The trained model is evaluated on unseen data to assess its generalization ability.

Performance Metrics

- Regression: Mean Squared Error (MSE), R-squared (R2R^2R2).

- Classification: Accuracy, Precision, Recall, F1-Score, ROC-AUC.

Popular Algorithms in Supervised Learning

Several algorithms underpin supervised learning, each with its strengths, weaknesses, and use cases. Here, we explore three fundamental algorithms: linear regression, decision trees, and SVMs.

1. Linear Regression

Linear regression is one of the simplest and most widely used algorithms for regression problems.

1.1 How It Works

- Linear regression models the relationship between input features (XXX) and the target variable (yyy) as a straight line: $y=\beta 0+\beta 1x1+\beta 2x2+...+\beta nxn$y = \beta_0 + \beta_1x_1 + \beta_2x_2 + \ldots + \beta_nx_ny$=\beta 0+\beta 1x1+\beta 2x2+...+\beta nxn$ Where:

  - $\beta 0$\beta_0$\beta 0$: Intercept.

  - $\beta 1,\beta 2,...$\beta_1, \beta_2, \ldots$\beta 1,\beta 2$,....: Coefficients for each feature.

1.2 Strengths

- Easy to interpret.

- Performs well with linearly separable data.

1.3 Weaknesses

- Poor performance on non-linear relationships.

- Sensitive to outliers.

1.4 Example: Predicting House Prices

- Features: Square footage, number of bedrooms, location.

- Label: Sale price.

- Model predicts prices using the equation learned from training data.

---

2. Decision Trees

Decision trees are versatile algorithms used for both regression and classification tasks.

2.1 How It Works

- A decision tree splits the data into subsets based on feature values, creating a tree-like structure where each leaf represents a prediction.

- Splitting criteria:

  - **Gini Impurity**: Measures how mixed the classes are in a node.

  - **Information Gain**: Evaluates the reduction in entropy after a split.

2.2 Strengths

- Intuitive and interpretable.

- Handles non-linear data well.

- Can work with both numerical and categorical data.

2.3 Weaknesses

- Prone to overfitting.

- Sensitive to small changes in data (high variance).

2.4 Example: Loan Approval System

- Features: Income, credit score, loan amount.

- Label: Approved or not approved.

- The decision tree predicts approval by following feature-based conditions.

3. Support Vector Machines (SVMs)

SVMs are powerful algorithms for both classification and regression tasks, particularly effective in high-dimensional spaces.

3.1 How It Works

- SVMs aim to find the hyperplane that best separates classes by maximizing the margin between the closest points (support vectors).

- **Kernel Trick**: Transforms data into higher dimensions to make it linearly separable using kernels like polynomial, radial basis function (RBF), or sigmoid.

3.2 Strengths

- Works well with small datasets and complex boundaries.

- Effective in high-dimensional spaces.

3.3 Weaknesses

- Computationally expensive with large datasets.

- Choosing the right kernel and hyperparameters can be challenging.

3.4 Example: Image Classification

- Features: Pixel intensity values.

- Label: Object categories (e.g., cat, dog, car).

- An SVM with an RBF kernel classifies images into predefined categories.

Practical Examples and Case Studies

Supervised learning's real-world applications span various industries. Let's explore practical examples and case studies that showcase its versatility.

1. Healthcare: Disease Diagnosis

Problem

Predict whether a patient has diabetes based on diagnostic measures like glucose level, BMI, and age.

Solution

- **Algorithm**: Logistic Regression.

- **Dataset**: Pima Indians Diabetes Dataset.

- **Steps**:

    1. Preprocess the data (e.g., handle missing values, scale features).

    2. Split into training and testing sets.

    3. Train a logistic regression model.

    4. Evaluate using accuracy, precision, and recall.

Outcome

The model achieves 85% accuracy, providing doctors with a reliable tool for early diagnosis.

---

2. Finance: Fraud Detection

Problem

Detect fraudulent credit card transactions based on spending patterns.

Solution

- **Algorithm**: Decision Tree or Random Forest.

- **Features**: Transaction amount, location, merchant type.

- **Steps**:

    1. Label historical transactions as "fraud" or "not fraud."

2. Train the model on labeled data.

3. Use feature importance to identify factors most associated with fraud.

Outcome

The model flags suspicious transactions for manual review, reducing financial losses.

---

3. Retail: Customer Churn Prediction

Problem

Predict whether a customer will stop using a subscription service based on usage patterns and demographic data.

Solution

- **Algorithm**: Support Vector Machine.

- **Features**: Number of logins, support tickets filed, monthly spending.

- **Steps**:

  1. Train an SVM with a radial basis function kernel.

  2. Use cross-validation to tune hyperparameters.

3. Deploy the model to predict churn probability for active customers.

Outcome

The company uses predictions to offer incentives to high-risk customers, improving retention rates by 20%.

---

4. Education: Personalized Learning

Problem

Classify students into learning groups based on their performance in assessments.

Solution

- **Algorithm**: K-Nearest Neighbors (KNN).

- **Features**: Test scores, participation levels, time spent on assignments.

- **Steps**:

  1. Assign labels to students based on learning styles (e.g., "visual," "auditory," "kinesthetic").

  2. Use KNN to classify new students into groups.

Outcome

Teachers tailor lesson plans to students' learning styles, improving overall performance.

Supervised learning is a cornerstone of machine learning, providing powerful tools to solve both regression and classification problems. By understanding the concepts of labels and outputs, practitioners can design models that generalize well to unseen data. Algorithms like linear regression, decision trees, and support vector machines demonstrate the diverse capabilities of supervised learning, each suited to specific tasks and datasets.

Practical examples from healthcare, finance, retail, and education highlight the tangible impact of supervised learning across industries. With its ability to address real-world challenges, supervised learning remains an essential skill for anyone seeking to harness the power of machine learning.

Chapter 6: Unsupervised Learning and Clustering Techniques

Unsupervised learning is a branch of machine learning that deals with data that has no labeled outputs. Unlike supervised learning, where the goal is to predict an outcome based on input features, unsupervised learning focuses on finding hidden patterns, structures, or relationships within the data. This makes it particularly useful for tasks like clustering, dimensionality reduction, and anomaly detection, where the insights are often exploratory in nature. In this chapter, we will delve deep into unsupervised learning, explore key clustering algorithms such as K-means, DBSCAN, and hierarchical clustering, understand dimensionality reduction techniques like PCA and t-SNE, and examine real-world use cases such as customer segmentation and anomaly detection.

Clustering Algorithms

Clustering is one of the most common techniques in unsupervised learning. It involves grouping similar data points into clusters based on their features. Let's explore some of the most popular clustering algorithms.

1. K-Means Clustering

Overview

K-means is a partition-based clustering algorithm that aims to divide a dataset into kkk clusters, where kkk is a predefined number. The algorithm works by minimizing the variance within each cluster while maximizing the variance between clusters.

How K-Means Works

1. **Initialization**: Select kkk random points as the initial centroids.

2. **Assignment Step**: Assign each data point to the nearest centroid based on a distance metric, usually Euclidean distance.

3. **Update Step**: Calculate the new centroid for each cluster as the mean of all points assigned to it.

4. **Repeat:** Iterate the assignment and update steps until the centroids stabilize or a predefined number of iterations is reached.

Strengths

- Simple to implement and computationally efficient.

- Works well for spherical or well-separated clusters.

Weaknesses

- Sensitive to the initial selection of centroids.

- Assumes clusters are of similar size and shape, which may not always be the case.

- Requires the number of clusters (kkk) to be predefined.

Applications

- Customer segmentation in marketing.

- Image compression by grouping similar pixel colors.

2. DBSCAN (Density-Based Spatial Clustering of Applications with Noise)

Overview

DBSCAN is a density-based clustering algorithm that groups data points closely packed together while marking points in low-density regions as noise.

How DBSCAN Works

1. Define two parameters:

    - **Epsilon (ε\varepsilon$\varepsilon$)**: The maximum distance between two points for them to be considered part of the same cluster.

    - **MinPts**: The minimum number of points required to form a dense region.

2. **Core Points**: Points with at least MinPts neighbors within ε\varepsilon$\varepsilon$.

3. **Border Points**: Points within ε\varepsilon$\varepsilon$ of a core point but with fewer than MinPts neighbors.

4. **Noise Points**: Points that are neither core nor border points.

5. The algorithm connects core points and their neighbors to form clusters.

Strengths

- Does not require the number of clusters to be specified beforehand.

- Can identify clusters of varying shapes and sizes.

- Handles noise and outliers effectively.

Weaknesses

- Sensitive to the choice of ε and MinPts.

- Struggles with datasets of varying densities.

Applications

- Anomaly detection in network security.

- Identifying geographical regions with similar attributes.

---

3. Hierarchical Clustering

Overview

Hierarchical clustering builds a hierarchy of clusters in either a bottom-up (agglomerative) or top-down (divisive) manner.

How Hierarchical Clustering Works

1. **Agglomerative Clustering**:

   o   Treat each data point as a separate cluster.

   o   Iteratively merge the closest clusters based on a distance metric until a single cluster remains.

2. **Divisive Clustering**:

   o   Start with all points in one cluster.

   o   Recursively split clusters until each data point forms its own cluster.

Linkage Criteria

- **Single Linkage**: Distance between the closest points in two clusters.

- **Complete Linkage**: Distance between the farthest points in two clusters.

- **Average Linkage**: Average distance between all points in two clusters.

Strengths

- Does not require the number of clusters to be specified beforehand.

- Provides a dendrogram (tree diagram) to visualize cluster relationships.

Weaknesses

- Computationally expensive for large datasets.

- Choice of linkage criteria can significantly impact results.

Applications

- Gene expression analysis in bioinformatics.

- Document clustering in text mining.

Dimensionality Reduction

In many datasets, the number of features can be overwhelming, leading to challenges in computation, visualization, and even model performance. Dimensionality reduction techniques help by reducing the number of features while retaining as much relevant information as possible.

1. Principal Component Analysis (PCA)

Overview

PCA is a linear dimensionality reduction technique that transforms the original features into a new set of orthogonal components, ranked by their variance.

How PCA Works

1. Standardize the dataset to have zero mean and unit variance.

2. Compute the covariance matrix to understand the relationships between features.

3. Calculate the eigenvectors and eigenvalues of the covariance matrix.

4. Select the top k eigenvectors corresponding to the largest eigenvalues to form the principal components.

Strengths

- Reduces dimensionality while preserving the most significant variance.

- Helps in noise reduction and visualization.

Weaknesses

- Assumes linear relationships between features.

- Loses interpretability as components are linear combinations of original features.

Applications

- Feature extraction in image recognition.

- Exploratory data analysis.

2. t-Distributed Stochastic Neighbor Embedding (t-SNE)

Overview

t-SNE is a non-linear dimensionality reduction technique designed for visualization by embedding high-dimensional data into a low-dimensional space (usually 2D or 3D).

How t-SNE Works

1. Measures the pairwise similarity of points in the high-dimensional space.

2. Projects the data into a lower-dimensional space while preserving the pairwise relationships as much as possible.

3. Uses gradient descent to minimize the difference between high-dimensional and low-dimensional representations.

Strengths

- Excellent for visualizing complex datasets.
- Captures non-linear structures that PCA may miss.

Weaknesses

- Computationally intensive for large datasets.

- Sensitive to hyperparameters like perplexity and learning rate.

Applications

- Visualizing clusters in high-dimensional datasets.

- Understanding feature relationships in neural networks.

Real-World Use Cases

Clustering and dimensionality reduction are not just theoretical concepts; they are widely applied across industries to solve real-world problems. Let's explore two prominent use cases.

1. Customer Segmentation

Overview

Businesses often have large datasets containing customer information, including demographics, purchase history, and browsing behavior. Clustering helps segment customers into distinct groups based on shared characteristics.

Process

1. Collect and preprocess customer data.

2. Use a clustering algorithm (e.g., K-means) to identify distinct customer segments.

3. Analyze clusters to understand customer preferences and behaviors.

Applications

- Targeted marketing campaigns tailored to specific segments.

- Personalized product recommendations.

- Identifying high-value customers for loyalty programs.

Example

An e-commerce company uses clustering to segment customers into groups like frequent buyers, deal-seekers, and first-time shoppers. By tailoring marketing strategies to each group, the company boosts customer satisfaction and sales.

---

2. Anomaly Detection

Overview

Anomaly detection identifies unusual patterns or data points that deviate significantly from the norm. It is particularly useful in detecting fraud, equipment failures, and security breaches.

Process

1. Train a clustering model (e.g., DBSCAN) on normal data.

2. Identify points that do not belong to any cluster as anomalies.

Applications

- Detecting fraudulent transactions in banking.

- Monitoring network traffic for cybersecurity threats.

- Predicting equipment failure in manufacturing.

Example

A bank uses clustering to analyze transaction patterns. Transactions that fall outside the usual clusters are flagged as potential fraud, allowing for timely intervention.

Unsupervised learning, particularly clustering and dimensionality reduction, is a powerful approach for discovering patterns and structures in unlabeled data. From customer segmentation to anomaly detection, these techniques have transformed how industries analyze and utilize data. By understanding algorithms like K-means, DBSCAN, and hierarchical clustering, along with tools like PCA and t-SNE, you can unlock valuable insights from even the most complex datasets. As you move forward, these foundational techniques will empower you to tackle real-world challenges and derive meaningful solutions.

Chapter 7: Deep Learning and Neural Networks

Deep learning has revolutionized machine learning and artificial intelligence (AI) by enabling computers to process and interpret vast amounts of complex data with unprecedented accuracy. At the heart of deep learning lies the neural network, a computational model inspired by the human brain. Neural networks power innovations such as autonomous vehicles, voice assistants, and cutting-edge medical diagnostics. This chapter will provide a comprehensive exploration of neural networks, their architecture, key concepts like activation functions and backpropagation, and the tools—TensorFlow and PyTorch—that make deep learning accessible to developers and researchers alike.

Introduction to Neural Networks and Their Architecture

What Are Neural Networks?

Neural networks are computational models that mimic the structure and function of the human brain. They consist of layers of interconnected nodes (also known as neurons) that process input data to produce an output. Each neuron applies mathematical operations to the data it receives, enabling the network to identify patterns, make predictions, or solve complex problems.

The Architecture of Neural Networks

The architecture of a neural network refers to the arrangement of its layers and neurons. Neural networks typically consist of three types of layers:

1. **Input Layer:**

    o   The input layer receives raw data and passes it to the next layer.

    o   Each node in this layer represents a single feature of the input data (e.g., pixel values in an image or attributes in a dataset).

2. **Hidden Layers:**

- o Hidden layers perform computations on the data using weighted connections and activation functions.

- o A network can have one or more hidden layers, and their number determines the network's depth (hence the term "deep learning").

3. **Output Layer**:

- o The output layer produces the final prediction or classification.

- o For example, in a classification task, this layer might output probabilities for different classes.

Connections and Weights

- Neurons in adjacent layers are connected by weighted edges. These weights determine the influence of one neuron on another.

- Adjusting the weights during training enables the network to learn from data.

Key Concepts in Neural Networks

To understand how neural networks function, it's essential to grasp the foundational concepts that govern their operation.

1. Activation Functions

Activation functions are mathematical functions applied to the output of a neuron to introduce non-linearity into the network. Non-linearity is crucial because most real-world data relationships are non-linear, and without it, neural networks would struggle to model complex patterns.

Common Activation Functions

1. **Sigmoid**:

   - Maps input values to a range between 0 and 1.

   - Commonly used in binary classification tasks.

   - Formula: σ(x)=11+e−x\sigma(x) = \frac{1}{1 + e^{-x}}σ(x)=1+e−x1

2. **ReLU (Rectified Linear Unit)**:

   - Outputs the input if it's positive; otherwise, it outputs zero.

- o Computationally efficient and helps mitigate the vanishing gradient problem.

- o Formula: $f(x) = \max(0, x)$

3. **Tanh**:

    - o Similar to sigmoid but maps values to a range between -1 and 1, providing stronger gradients.

    - o Formula:
      $$\tanh(x) = \frac{e^x - e^{-x}}{e^x + e^{-x}}$$

4. **Softmax**:

    - o Converts raw outputs into probabilities that sum to 1, making it ideal for multi-class classification tasks.

    - o Formula:
      $$\text{softmax}(x_i) = \frac{e^{x_i}}{\sum_{j} e^{x_j}}$$

2. Backpropagation

Backpropagation is the algorithm that enables neural networks to learn by adjusting weights and biases. It works by calculating the gradient of the loss function with respect to each weight, then updating the weights to minimize the loss.

Steps in Backpropagation

1. **Forward Pass**:

    o Data flows through the network, and predictions are made.

    o The loss (difference between predicted and actual values) is calculated using a loss function (e.g., Mean Squared Error for regression or Cross-Entropy for classification).

2. **Backward Pass**:

    o The loss is propagated backward through the network to compute the gradients of the loss function with respect to each weight.

    o The chain rule of calculus is used to compute these gradients layer by layer.

3. **Weight Update**:

- o The gradients are used to update weights via an optimization algorithm (e.g., gradient descent).

---

3. Layers in Neural Networks

Neural networks can be categorized based on the type and arrangement of layers:

Fully Connected Layers (Dense Layers)

- Every neuron in one layer is connected to every neuron in the next layer.

- Common in feedforward neural networks.

Convolutional Layers (CNNs)

- Used in image processing tasks.

- Detect features like edges, textures, or objects by applying convolutional filters.

Recurrent Layers (RNNs)

- Designed for sequential data like time series or text.

- Maintain memory of previous inputs, making them suitable for language modeling and speech recognition.

Tools for Deep Learning: TensorFlow and PyTorch Basics

Modern deep learning frameworks like TensorFlow and PyTorch have made it easier than ever to build, train, and deploy neural networks. Both are open-source, widely adopted, and supported by robust ecosystems.

TensorFlow

TensorFlow, developed by Google Brain, is one of the most popular deep learning frameworks. It provides a flexible platform for designing, training, and deploying ML models.

Key Features

- **TensorFlow Core**: Offers low-level functionality for building custom models.

- **Keras API**: A high-level API integrated into TensorFlow, making it easier to design and train models.

- **TensorFlow Lite**: Supports deploying models on mobile and edge devices.

Basic Workflow

1. **Define the Model**: Use the Sequential API or functional API to specify the network architecture.

python

```
import tensorflow as tf

model = tf.keras.Sequential([
    tf.keras.layers.Dense(64, activation='relu'),
    tf.keras.layers.Dense(10, activation='softmax')
])
```

2. **Compile the Model**: Specify the optimizer, loss function, and evaluation metrics.

python

```
model.compile(optimizer='adam',
loss='sparse_categorical_crossentropy',
metrics=['accuracy'])
```

3. **Train the Model**: Fit the model to the training data.

python

```
model.fit(X_train, y_train, epochs=10,
batch_size=32)
```

PyTorch

PyTorch, developed by Facebook's AI Research lab, is another leading framework known for its dynamic computation graph, which allows more flexibility during model training.

Key Features

- **Dynamic Graphs**: Compute the graph during runtime, enabling easier debugging.

- **TorchScript**: Converts models to deployable formats.

- **Built-In Support for GPUs**: Simplifies hardware acceleration.

Basic Workflow

1. **Define the Model**: Use the torch.nn module to specify the architecture.

python

```python
import torch

import torch.nn as nn


class NeuralNet(nn.Module):
    def __init__(self):
        super(NeuralNet, self).__init__()
        self.fc1 = nn.Linear(64, 128)
        self.fc2 = nn.Linear(128, 10)


    def forward(self, x):
        x = torch.relu(self.fc1(x))
        x = torch.softmax(self.fc2(x), dim=1)
        return x
```

2. **Define the Loss and Optimizer:**

python

```python
criterion = nn.CrossEntropyLoss()
optimizer = torch.optim.Adam(model.parameters(), lr=0.001)
```

3. **Train the Model**: Use a training loop to iterate through batches of data.

```python
python

for epoch in range(epochs):
    optimizer.zero_grad()
    outputs = model(X_train)
    loss = criterion(outputs, y_train)
    loss.backward()
    optimizer.step()
```

Deep learning and neural networks have transformed how we approach complex data problems, enabling breakthroughs across industries. Neural networks, with their layered architecture, activation functions, and backpropagation, provide a robust framework for learning patterns from data. Tools like TensorFlow and PyTorch have democratized deep learning, making it accessible to developers and researchers worldwide. By mastering these fundamentals, you'll be equipped to build and deploy powerful deep learning models, paving the way for innovative solutions to real-world challenges.

Chapter 8: Feature Engineering

Machine learning models are only as good as the data they are trained on. While algorithms and frameworks receive significant attention, the quality and relevance of the input features often play an even greater role in determining model performance. This is where **feature engineering** becomes crucial. It is the art and science of transforming raw data into meaningful features that can improve the predictive power of machine learning models. In this chapter, we will explore the critical importance of feature engineering, delve into common transformation techniques, and examine how automation is reshaping the landscape of feature selection.

What is Feature Engineering and Why is it Critical?

Feature engineering is the process of selecting, creating, and transforming input variables to enhance the performance of machine learning models. It involves converting raw data into a format that is better suited for analysis and prediction.

Why is Feature Engineering Essential?

1. Improves Model Performance

- The quality of features often determines how effectively an algorithm learns patterns in the data. Poor features can lead to underperforming models, while well-crafted features can significantly boost accuracy and robustness.

- For example, in predicting house prices, a feature such as "price per square foot" may be more predictive than just using "price" and "square footage" as separate variables.

2. Reduces Model Complexity

- By engineering meaningful features, you can reduce the need for complex algorithms. A simple model trained on well-engineered features often outperforms a complex model trained on raw data.

- Simplified models are easier to interpret and deploy.

3. Mitigates Overfitting and Underfitting

- Good features help capture the underlying patterns in data, reducing the risk of overfitting (memorizing noise) or underfitting (failing to learn).

- For instance, encoding time-related information (like month, season, or day of the week) can capture trends in sales data without overfitting.

4. Enables Use of Diverse Data Types

- Raw data often comes in different formats, such as text, images, or timestamps. Feature engineering bridges the gap, allowing machine learning algorithms to process and learn from these diverse data types.

5. Adds Domain Knowledge

- Feature engineering allows you to incorporate domain-specific insights into the model. For example, in healthcare, combining symptoms into clinical scores can provide more predictive features than raw symptom counts.

In summary, feature engineering is the bridge between raw data and actionable insights. It empowers machine learning models to perform better by focusing on the most relevant and meaningful aspects of the data.

Common Feature Transformation Techniques

Feature transformation involves modifying existing features to make them more useful for the model. This step is integral to the feature engineering process and includes techniques such as scaling, encoding, creating new features, and more.

1. Scaling and Normalization

Why It Matters

- Many machine learning algorithms, such as support vector machines (SVMs) and k-nearest neighbors (KNN), are sensitive to the scale of input features. Features with larger ranges can dominate those with smaller ranges.

Techniques

1. **Min-Max Scaling:**

    o   Transforms features to a range between 0 and 1.

- o Formula:
  $X'=X-\min(X)\max(X)-\min(X)X' = \frac{X - \min(X)}{\max(X) - \min(X)}X'=\max(X)-\min(X)X-\min(X)$

2. **Standardization (Z-Score Normalization):**

   - o Centers data by subtracting the mean and scales it by dividing by the standard deviation.

   - o Formula: $Z=X-\mu\sigma Z = \frac{X - \mu}{\sigma}Z=\sigma X-\mu$

3. **Log Transformation:**

   - o Reduces the impact of extreme values by compressing the range of data.

   - o Commonly used for features with skewed distributions, like income or sales.

---

2. Encoding Categorical Variables

Categorical data must be converted into numerical representations for most machine learning algorithms to process it effectively.

Techniques

1. **One-Hot Encoding**:

   o Creates binary columns for each category in a feature.

   o Example: If "Color" has values ["Red", "Blue", "Green"], one-hot encoding creates three binary features: "Color_Red," "Color_Blue," and "Color_Green."

2. **Label Encoding**:

   o Assigns integer values to categories.

   o Example: "Red" = 1, "Blue" = 2, "Green" = 3.

3. **Frequency Encoding**:

   o Replaces each category with its frequency or count in the dataset.

   o Example: If "Blue" appears 50 times and "Red" appears 30 times, these are replaced with 50 and 30, respectively.

3. Handling Missing Values

Missing data can lead to biased models or errors during training. Properly handling missing values is crucial in feature engineering.

Techniques

1. **Imputation**:

   o Replace missing values with a statistic like the mean, median, or mode.

   o Example: Replace missing ages in a dataset with the median age.

2. **Indicator Variable**:

   o Create a binary column to indicate whether a value was missing.

3. **Model-Based Imputation**:

   o Use a regression model to predict missing values based on other features.

---

4. Feature Creation

Creating new features often adds more predictive power to the model. This step leverages domain knowledge or existing relationships in the data.

Techniques

1. **Mathematical Combinations**:

   o Combine features using mathematical operations.

   o Example: Combine "Height" and "Weight" to create "BMI."

2. **Date and Time Features**:

   o Extract features like day of the week, month, or time of day from timestamp data.

3. **Text Features**:

   o Use Natural Language Processing (NLP) techniques to create features like word counts, sentiment scores, or TF-IDF (Term Frequency-Inverse Document Frequency).

4. **Interaction Features**:

   o Create features that represent interactions between two or more existing features.

   o Example: Multiply "Price" and "Quantity" to create "Total Revenue."

5. Feature Reduction

Sometimes, too many features can lead to overfitting or high computational costs. Reducing the number of features helps simplify the model without significant loss of information.

Techniques

1. **Principal Component Analysis (PCA):**

   o Reduces dimensionality by transforming features into principal components that capture the most variance in the data.

2. **Feature Aggregation:**

   o Combine multiple features into a single representative feature.

   o Example: Use the average of monthly sales as a single "average sales" feature.

Automating Feature Selection

Feature selection involves identifying the most relevant features from the dataset to improve model performance and efficiency. While traditionally manual, automation is becoming increasingly popular, thanks to advancements in machine learning tools and libraries.

Why Automate Feature Selection?

1. **Scalability**:

   - Modern datasets can contain thousands of features. Manual selection is impractical for large-scale data.

2. **Objectivity**:

   - Automation reduces human bias in selecting features.

3. **Efficiency**:

   - Speeds up the data preprocessing pipeline, allowing faster experimentation.

Techniques for Automated Feature Selection

1. Filter Methods

- Rank features based on statistical measures and select the top-performing ones.

Examples:

1. **Correlation Coefficients**:
   - Identify features strongly correlated with the target variable.

2. **Chi-Square Test**:
   - Evaluate the independence between categorical features and the target.

---

2. Wrapper Methods

- Use machine learning models to evaluate subsets of features and iteratively select the best combination.

Examples:

1. **Recursive Feature Elimination (RFE)**:
   - Removes the least important features one by one and evaluates model performance.

2. **Stepwise Selection**:
   - Adds or removes features iteratively based on their contribution to model accuracy.

---

3. Embedded Methods

- Feature selection is integrated directly into the training process of certain algorithms.

Examples:

1. **Lasso Regression**:

   o Shrinks less important feature coefficients to zero, effectively performing feature selection.

2. **Tree-Based Methods**:

   o Decision trees and ensemble models like Random Forests provide feature importance scores.

Modern Tools for Feature Engineering Automation

1. **Featuretools**:

   o An open-source Python library for automated feature engineering. It creates new features by applying predefined transformation and aggregation rules.

2. **AutoML Platforms**:

- Tools like H2O.ai and Google AutoML include automated feature selection as part of their pipeline.

3. **Scikit-learn:**

   - Provides built-in methods for feature selection, such as SelectKBest and VarianceThreshold.

Feature engineering is a critical step in the machine learning workflow, often determining the difference between a mediocre model and a highly accurate one. By transforming raw data into meaningful features, engineers and data scientists can unlock the full potential of machine learning algorithms. With the rise of automation, feature engineering is becoming more efficient, allowing practitioners to focus on solving complex problems. By mastering these techniques and leveraging modern tools, you will be well-equipped to tackle real-world challenges and build models that deliver powerful insights.

Chapter 9: Model Evaluation and Validation

Building a machine learning model is only part of the journey. Evaluating its performance and ensuring it generalizes well to unseen data is equally, if not more, important. A well-trained model should strike a balance between capturing the underlying patterns in the data while avoiding noise and overcomplication. In this chapter, we will explore the concepts of overfitting and underfitting, discuss evaluation metrics for both classification and regression tasks, and dive into cross-validation techniques to ensure reliable model performance.

Overfitting and Underfitting: How to Identify and Fix Them

Overfitting and underfitting are two common issues encountered when training machine learning models. Both problems stem from the model's ability—or lack thereof—to generalize beyond the training data.

Overfitting: When the Model Learns Too Much

Overfitting occurs when a model captures not only the underlying patterns in the data but also noise and random fluctuations. This leads to excellent performance on the training data but poor generalization to unseen data.

Symptoms of Overfitting

1. **High Training Accuracy, Low Validation Accuracy**: The model performs extremely well on the training set but poorly on the validation or test set.

2. **Complex Decision Boundaries**: For classification tasks, the decision boundaries might be overly complex, trying to accommodate every training data point.

How to Fix Overfitting

1. **Simplify the Model**:

   - Reduce the number of parameters or layers in the model.

   - For example, in neural networks, use fewer hidden units or layers.

2. **Regularization**:

- o Add a penalty term to the loss function to discourage overly complex models.

- o Techniques:

  - **L1 Regularization**: Encourages sparsity by penalizing the absolute values of weights.

  - **L2 Regularization**: Penalizes the square of the weights, making them smaller.

3. **Add More Training Data**:

   - o Increasing the size and diversity of the training dataset helps the model generalize better.

4. **Data Augmentation**:

   - o Generate synthetic data by applying transformations like rotation, flipping, or cropping (useful for image data).

5. **Early Stopping**:

   - o Monitor the model's performance on the validation set during training and stop when performance no longer improves.

Underfitting: When the Model Learns Too Little

Underfitting occurs when a model is too simple to capture the underlying patterns in the data. It performs poorly on both the training and validation datasets.

Symptoms of Underfitting

1. **Low Training Accuracy**: The model fails to learn even the basic structure of the data.

2. **High Bias**: Predictions are consistently off, indicating a lack of flexibility in the model.

How to Fix Underfitting

1. **Increase Model Complexity**:

   o Use more complex algorithms or increase the number of parameters.

   o For example, switch from linear regression to polynomial regression.

2. **Reduce Regularization**:

   o Excessive regularization can oversimplify the model. Adjust the regularization parameters to allow more flexibility.

3. **Feature Engineering**:

o Create additional features or transform existing ones to provide the model with more information.

4. **Train for Longer:**

o Extend the training duration or use a lower learning rate to allow the model to converge.

By identifying and addressing overfitting and underfitting, you can build models that strike the right balance between complexity and generalization.

Evaluation Metrics for Classification and Regression Tasks

Evaluating a machine learning model requires metrics tailored to the task at hand. Whether it's predicting labels (classification) or continuous values (regression), selecting the right metric ensures a comprehensive understanding of the model's performance.

Evaluation Metrics for Classification Tasks

Classification involves predicting discrete labels, such as determining whether an email is spam or not. Key metrics include:

1. Accuracy

- The percentage of correctly classified instances out of the total instances.

- Formula:

Accuracy=True Positives (TP)+True Negatives (TN)Total Samples\text{Accuracy} = \frac{\text{True Positives (TP)} + \text{True Negatives (TN)}}{\text{Total Samples}}Accuracy=Total SamplesTrue Positives (TP)+True Negatives (TN)

- **Limitations**:

  - Not ideal for imbalanced datasets (e.g., where one class significantly outweighs another).

---

2. Precision, Recall, and F1-Score

1. **Precision**:

   - Measures the proportion of true positives out of all predicted positives.

- Formula:
  $$\text{Precision} = \frac{\text{TP}}{\text{TP} + \text{False Positives (FP)}}$$

- High precision means fewer false positives.

2. Recall (Sensitivity):

- Measures the proportion of true positives out of all actual positives.

- Formula:
  $$\text{Recall} = \frac{\text{TP}}{\text{TP} + \text{False Negatives (FN)}}$$

- High recall means fewer false negatives.

3. F1-Score:

- The harmonic mean of precision and recall.

- Formula: $\text{F1-Score} = 2 \cdot$

\frac{\text{Precision} \cdot \text{Recall}}{\text{Precision} + \text{Recall}}F1- Score=2·Precision+RecallPrecision·Re call

- o Useful for imbalanced datasets.

---

3. ROC-AUC (Receiver Operating Characteristic – Area Under Curve)

- Evaluates the trade-off between true positive rate (sensitivity) and false positive rate.

- A higher AUC indicates better model performance.

Evaluation Metrics for Regression Tasks

Regression models predict continuous values, such as house prices or temperature. Key metrics include:

1. Mean Absolute Error (MAE)

- Measures the average magnitude of errors in predictions, without considering their direction.

- Formula: MAE=1n∑i=1n|yi−y^i|\text{MAE} = \frac{1}{n} \sum_{i=1}^n |y_i - \hat{y}_i|MAE=n1i=1∑n|yi−y^i|

- Easy to interpret but does not penalize large errors heavily.

---

2. Mean Squared Error (MSE)

- Measures the average squared difference between predicted and actual values.

- Formula: MSE=1n∑i=1n(yi−y^i)2\text{MSE} = \frac{1}{n} \sum_{i=1}^n (y_i - \hat{y}_i)^2MSE=n1i=1∑n(yi−y^i)2

- Penalizes large errors more than MAE.

---

3. Root Mean Squared Error (RMSE)

- The square root of MSE, providing errors in the same unit as the target variable.

- Formula: RMSE=MSE\text{RMSE} = \sqrt{\text{MSE}}RMSE=MSE

---

4. R-Squared (R2R^2R2)

- Indicates the proportion of variance in the dependent variable that is predictable from the independent variables.

- Formula:
  R2=1−∑i=1n(yi−y^i)2∑i=1n(yi−y‾)2R^2 = 1 - \frac{\sum_{i=1}^n (y_i - \hat{y}_i)^2}{\sum_{i=1}^n (y_i - \bar{y})^2}R2=1−∑i=1n(yi−y‾)2∑i=1n(yi−y^i)2

Cross-Validation Techniques

Cross-validation is a statistical method used to evaluate model performance by splitting the data into training and testing subsets. This technique ensures that the model generalizes well to unseen data.

---

1. Holdout Validation

- Splits the dataset into a training set and a test set.

- Commonly used split ratios are 80:20 or 70:30.

- **Limitation**: Model performance depends on the specific split, which may not be representative of the overall data distribution.

---

2. K-Fold Cross-Validation

- Divides the dataset into k subsets (folds).

- The model is trained on $k-1$ folds and validated on the remaining fold. This process is repeated k times, with each fold serving as the validation set once.

- **Advantages**: Reduces variability by averaging the results across folds.

---

3. Stratified K-Fold Cross-Validation

- A variant of K-fold cross-validation that ensures each fold has a proportional representation of classes.

- Useful for imbalanced datasets.

---

4. Leave-One-Out Cross-Validation (LOOCV)

- Uses a single instance as the test set and the rest as the training set.

- Repeated for every data point.

- **Limitation**: Computationally expensive for large datasets.

---

5. Time Series Cross-Validation

- For time-dependent data, splits must respect the temporal order to prevent data leakage.

- Common approach: Rolling window or expanding window validation.

Model evaluation and validation are indispensable steps in the machine learning pipeline. Understanding overfitting and underfitting allows you to diagnose and address performance issues effectively. Selecting the right evaluation metric ensures that the model is aligned with the specific goals of your task, whether classification or regression. Finally, cross-validation techniques provide a robust framework for assessing model generalization, ensuring reliability and trustworthiness in real-world applications. By mastering these principles, you will be well-equipped to build models that not only perform well but also stand up to scrutiny in diverse scenarios.

Chapter 10: Natural Language Processing (NLP)

Natural Language Processing (NLP) bridges the gap between human communication and machine understanding. As a subfield of artificial intelligence (AI), NLP focuses on enabling machines to read, interpret, and generate human language. From chatbots and sentiment analysis to machine translation and voice recognition, NLP has revolutionized the way we interact with technology. In this chapter, we'll explore the fundamentals of NLP, delve into essential preprocessing techniques like tokenization, stemming, and lemmatization, and examine real-world applications that demonstrate the transformative power of NLP.

Basics of NLP and Text Preprocessing

What is NLP?

NLP involves developing algorithms that allow machines to process, analyze, and generate natural language. Unlike structured data, human language is complex and often ambiguous, requiring a combination of linguistic knowledge and computational techniques to make sense of it.

Key Challenges in NLP

1. **Ambiguity:**

   o Words and phrases can have multiple meanings depending on context.

   o Example: "Bank" could refer to a financial institution or the side of a river.

2. **Syntax vs. Semantics:**

   o Syntax focuses on the structure of sentences, while semantics deals with their meaning. NLP must account for both.

3. **Language Variability:**

   o Dialects, slang, and regional differences add layers of complexity.

4. **Unstructured Data:**

   o Most language data, like emails or tweets, is unstructured, requiring extensive preprocessing.

Text Preprocessing in NLP

Text preprocessing is the foundational step in NLP pipelines. It involves preparing raw text for analysis by cleaning and standardizing it, ensuring that algorithms can effectively process the data.

Common Steps in Text Preprocessing

1. **Text Cleaning**:
   - Remove noise such as special characters, punctuation, and extra whitespace.
   - Example: "Hello!! How are you???" becomes "Hello How are you".

2. **Lowercasing**:
   - Convert all text to lowercase for uniformity.
   - Example: "Apple" and "apple" are treated as the same word.

3. **Removing Stop Words**:
   - Eliminate common words like "and," "the," or "is" that don't contribute much meaning.

4. **Handling Numbers and Symbols**:

○ Decide whether to retain, replace, or remove numeric values and special symbols based on the task.

5. **Text Normalization:**

○ Standardize text by correcting misspellings or expanding contractions.

○ Example: "u r" becomes "you are."

Preprocessing ensures that data is clean, consistent, and ready for the next stages of analysis.

Techniques: Tokenization, Stemming, and Lemmatization

Text preprocessing involves breaking down and transforming text into formats suitable for machine learning algorithms. Three fundamental techniques in this process are tokenization, stemming, and lemmatization.

1. Tokenization

What is Tokenization?

Tokenization is the process of splitting text into smaller units, or tokens. These tokens could be words, phrases, or even individual characters, depending on the use case.

Types of Tokenization

1. **Word Tokenization**:

   o Splits text into words.

   o Example: "Natural Language Processing is fun" → ["Natural", "Language", "Processing", "is", "fun"].

2. **Sentence Tokenization**:

   o Splits text into sentences.

   o Example: "NLP is fascinating. It has many applications." → ["NLP is fascinating.", "It has many applications."].

3. **Subword Tokenization**:

   o Breaks words into smaller units, often used in modern NLP models like BERT and GPT.

○ Example: "unbelievable" → ["un", "believ", "able"].

Why is Tokenization Important?

- Tokenization transforms raw text into manageable units for further analysis.

- It preserves the structure of text while enabling algorithms to focus on individual elements.

---

2. Stemming

What is Stemming?

Stemming reduces words to their root or base form, often by stripping affixes like prefixes and suffixes. The resulting stem may not always be a valid word.

Example:

- Words: "running," "runs," "runner" → Stem: "run".

Popular Stemming Algorithms

1. **Porter Stemmer:**

   ○ Widely used, rule-based algorithm.

2. **Snowball Stemmer:**

  - More advanced and accurate than the Porter stemmer.

Advantages

- Reduces vocabulary size, improving computational efficiency.

Limitations

- Sometimes results in overly aggressive reductions.

- Example: "university" → "univers".

---

3. Lemmatization

What is Lemmatization?

Lemmatization is a more sophisticated technique that reduces words to their base or dictionary form (lemma) while considering context and grammar.

Example:

- Words: "running," "ran," "runs" → Lemma: "run".

How it Works

- Lemmatization uses linguistic knowledge, such as part-of-speech tags, to ensure accuracy.

Advantages

- Produces valid words, making it more meaningful than stemming.

Limitations

- Computationally intensive compared to stemming.

Stemming vs. Lemmatization

Aspect	Stemming	Lemmatization
Approach	Rule-based	Linguistic knowledge
Output	May not be a valid word	Always a valid word
Speed	Faster	Slower
Accuracy	Less accurate	More accurate

Both techniques have their place in NLP pipelines, depending on the task and required precision.

Real-World NLP Applications

The real-world impact of NLP is vast and spans across industries. Below are some of the most transformative applications:

1. Chatbots and Virtual Assistants

Overview

- Chatbots like ChatGPT and virtual assistants like Siri, Alexa, and Google Assistant use NLP to understand and respond to user queries.

How It Works

1. Speech recognition converts spoken words into text.

2. NLP analyzes the text to determine intent and extract key information.

3. The system generates appropriate responses using text generation models.

Applications

- Customer support: Automating FAQs and troubleshooting.

- Smart home control: Interpreting voice commands for devices.

---

2. Sentiment Analysis

Overview

- Sentiment analysis determines whether a piece of text expresses positive, negative, or neutral sentiment.

How It Works

- NLP models classify text based on sentiment indicators like words ("happy," "terrible") and context.

Applications

- Monitoring social media sentiment about products or brands.
- Analyzing customer reviews to gauge satisfaction.

Example

A restaurant uses sentiment analysis to process Yelp reviews and identify recurring customer complaints.

---

3. Machine Translation

Overview

- Machine translation systems like Google Translate convert text from one language to another.

How It Works

- NLP models analyze syntax, semantics, and context to produce fluent translations.

Applications

- Bridging language barriers in global communication.

- Real-time subtitles for videos and meetings.

Example

A multinational company uses machine translation to communicate with teams across different countries.

---

4. Text Summarization

Overview

- Summarization condenses long documents into shorter, meaningful summaries.

How It Works

1. **Extractive Summarization**: Selects key sentences from the original text.

2. **Abstractive Summarization**: Generates summaries in new words while preserving meaning.

Applications

- Summarizing news articles or legal documents.

- Creating concise meeting notes.

5. Healthcare Applications

Overview

- NLP is transforming healthcare by enabling the analysis of unstructured medical records and improving patient care.

Applications

- Extracting critical information from patient notes.

- Assisting in medical diagnoses through symptom analysis.

Example

NLP-powered systems help physicians identify potential drug interactions by analyzing patient histories.

6. Search Engines

Overview

- Search engines like Google and Bing use NLP to improve query understanding and provide relevant results.

How It Works

- NLP algorithms analyze search queries, infer user intent, and rank results based on relevance.

Applications

- Personalized search recommendations.

- Voice-based search using natural language.

---

7. Anomaly Detection

Overview

- NLP is used to detect anomalies in text data, such as fraud or unusual activity.

Applications

- Identifying phishing emails in cybersecurity.

- Spotting irregular patterns in financial transactions.

Natural Language Processing is at the heart of modern AI systems, enabling machines to process, understand, and generate human language with remarkable accuracy. By mastering foundational techniques like tokenization, stemming, and lemmatization, and understanding their real-world applications, we can unlock the true potential of NLP. From chatbots and machine translation to sentiment analysis and healthcare advancements, NLP continues to redefine how we interact with technology and each other. With its growing capabilities, the future of NLP holds immense possibilities for innovation and impact.

Chapter 11: Computer Vision

Computer Vision is a transformative field within artificial intelligence (AI) that enables machines to interpret and make decisions based on visual data. It combines principles of image processing, machine learning, and deep learning to analyze images and videos, mimicking the human ability to see and understand the world. With applications ranging from autonomous vehicles to facial recognition, computer vision is at the forefront of technological innovation. In this chapter, we'll explore the foundations of computer vision, delve into Convolutional Neural Networks (CNNs)—the backbone of modern vision systems—and examine practical applications like object detection and facial recognition.

Introduction to Image Processing and Computer Vision

What is Computer Vision?

Computer Vision focuses on enabling computers to "see" and understand images and videos. While humans effortlessly interpret visual data, teaching machines to do the same requires advanced algorithms and techniques. The goal is to replicate human vision processes and apply them to a wide array of tasks.

Key Goals of Computer Vision

1. **Recognition**: Identify objects, people, or scenes in images.

2. **Detection**: Locate specific objects within an image or video.

3. **Segmentation**: Partition an image into regions or objects for analysis.

4. **Tracking**: Monitor objects across frames in a video.

How Does Image Processing Relate to Computer Vision?

Image processing refers to the manipulation and analysis of digital images to enhance their quality or extract information. While image processing is more about modifying or improving images, computer vision focuses on understanding and interpreting them.

Common Image Processing Techniques

1. **Filtering**: Remove noise or highlight features using techniques like Gaussian or median filtering.

2. **Edge Detection**: Identify boundaries within an image using algorithms like Canny or Sobel.

3. **Histogram Equalization**: Improve contrast by redistributing pixel intensity values.

4. **Thresholding**: Segment an image by converting it into binary format based on intensity.

Image processing serves as a preprocessing step for computer vision tasks, ensuring that the data is clean and structured before further analysis.

Convolutional Neural Networks (CNNs) Explained

Traditional machine learning methods struggle with raw image data due to its high dimensionality and complexity. Convolutional Neural Networks (CNNs) address this challenge by leveraging specialized architectures designed for image data.

What is a CNN?

A CNN is a type of deep learning model specifically designed for processing grid-like data, such as images. It automatically extracts hierarchical features from raw pixel data, enabling powerful and scalable solutions for image-related tasks.

Key Components of a CNN

1. Convolutional Layers

The convolutional layer is the heart of a CNN. It applies filters (kernels) to the input image to extract features like edges, textures, or patterns.

- **How It Works:**
  - A filter slides over the input image, performing element-wise multiplication and summing the results.

o   The output is called a feature map.

- **Example**:
  For a filter detecting horizontal edges, bright regions in the feature map represent areas with strong horizontal patterns.

2. Activation Functions

Introduce non-linearity to the model, allowing it to learn complex patterns. The most commonly used activation function in CNNs is the **ReLU (Rectified Linear Unit)**.

- **Formula**: $f(x)=\max(0,x)$ $f(x) = \max(0, x)$ $f(x)=\max(0,x)$

- **Purpose**: Discards negative values, retaining only positive signals.

3. Pooling Layers

Pooling layers reduce the spatial dimensions of the feature maps, making computations more efficient and reducing overfitting.

- **Types of Pooling**:

  o   **Max Pooling**: Takes the maximum value in a region.

  o   **Average Pooling**: Computes the average value in a region.

- **Example**:
  A 2x2 max pooling operation on a feature map retains the most significant value in each 2x2 region.

4. Fully Connected Layers

These layers connect every neuron from one layer to every neuron in the next. Fully connected layers aggregate the features extracted by convolutional and pooling layers to make final predictions.

5. Dropout

Dropout is a regularization technique that randomly disables neurons during training, preventing overfitting and improving generalization.

How CNNs Learn

CNNs learn through a process called backpropagation, which adjusts the weights of the filters to minimize the error between predictions and actual labels. Key steps include:

1. **Forward Propagation**: Input passes through the network, generating predictions.

2. **Loss Calculation**: Compute the difference between predictions and ground truth using a loss function (e.g., cross-entropy for classification tasks).

3. **Backward Propagation**: Gradients of the loss function with respect to each parameter are computed and used to update the weights.

Advantages of CNNs

- Automatically learns features, eliminating the need for manual feature engineering.

- Captures spatial hierarchies, recognizing simple patterns (edges) in early layers and complex patterns (shapes) in deeper layers.

- Scalable for large datasets and complex tasks.

Practical Applications of Computer Vision

Computer Vision has moved beyond research labs to power real-world systems across industries. Let's explore two key applications: object detection and facial recognition.

---

1. Object Detection

Object detection combines classification and localization, enabling systems to identify objects in an image and pinpoint their locations using bounding boxes.

How Object Detection Works

1. **Feature Extraction**:

   o A CNN extracts features from the input image.

2. **Region Proposal**:

   o Regions likely to contain objects are identified. Algorithms like Selective Search or Region Proposal Networks (RPNs) are commonly used.

3. **Classification and Localization**:

   o Each proposed region is classified, and bounding box coordinates are predicted.

Popular Object Detection Models

1. **YOLO (You Only Look Once)**:

   o Processes an image in a single pass, making it extremely fast.

- o Suitable for real-time applications like autonomous driving.

2. **Faster R-CNN:**

    - o Combines region proposals with CNN-based classification for high accuracy.

3. **SSD (Single Shot MultiBox Detector):**

    - o Balances speed and accuracy, making it ideal for mobile devices.

Applications of Object Detection

- **Autonomous Vehicles**: Detect pedestrians, vehicles, and road signs in real-time.

- **Retail**: Track inventory and detect misplaced items in stores.

- **Healthcare**: Identify abnormalities in medical scans, such as tumors.

---

2. Facial Recognition

Facial recognition systems identify or verify individuals based on their facial features. They are widely used in security, authentication, and social media platforms.

How Facial Recognition Works

1. **Face Detection:**

   o The system first detects faces in an image or video. Algorithms like Haar Cascades or deep learning-based methods (e.g., MTCNN) are commonly used.

2. **Feature Extraction:**

   o Key facial landmarks (eyes, nose, mouth) are identified.

   o CNNs extract distinguishing features for further analysis.

3. **Face Matching:**

   o Extracted features are compared against a database of known faces using similarity metrics like cosine similarity or Euclidean distance.

Challenges in Facial Recognition

- Variations in lighting, pose, and expressions.

- Occlusions (e.g., sunglasses, masks).

- Ethical concerns, such as privacy and bias.

Applications of Facial Recognition

- **Security**: Authenticate users for devices and access control systems.

- **Law Enforcement**: Identify suspects from surveillance footage.

- **Personalization**: Social media platforms use it for tagging friends in photos.

Other Real-World Applications of Computer Vision

Healthcare

- Diagnose diseases from X-rays, MRIs, and CT scans.

- Track patient recovery through visual data analysis.

Agriculture

- Monitor crop health using drones equipped with computer vision systems.

- Detect pests and diseases early for targeted intervention.

Manufacturing

- Perform quality control by identifying defects in products.

- Automate assembly line operations through visual inspection.

Entertainment

- Power augmented reality (AR) experiences, such as Snapchat filters.

- Create realistic visual effects in movies and games.

Computer Vision is a rapidly evolving field that empowers machines to analyze and understand visual data at a scale and precision unattainable by humans. By leveraging techniques like image processing and Convolutional Neural Networks (CNNs), it has become the driving force behind applications like object detection, facial recognition, and beyond. As computer vision continues to advance, its potential to transform industries—from healthcare and security to entertainment and transportation—remains boundless. By mastering its foundations and practical applications, you can contribute to shaping a future where machines "see" the world as we do.

Chapter 12: Reinforcement Learning

Reinforcement Learning (RL) is a captivating subfield of machine learning where agents learn to make decisions by interacting with an environment to maximize a cumulative reward. Unlike supervised learning, where models learn from labeled data, or unsupervised learning, which focuses on uncovering patterns, RL revolves around sequential decision-making in uncertain and dynamic environments. From training robots to perform complex tasks to mastering games like Chess and Go, RL is driving innovation across industries. In this chapter, we'll explore the basics of reward-based learning, dive into key RL algorithms such as Q-learning and policy gradients, and examine practical applications in robotics, gaming, and resource optimization.

The Basics of Reward-Based Learning

Reinforcement Learning draws inspiration from behavioral psychology, where an agent (like a human or animal) learns through trial and error, guided by rewards or penalties. The agent's goal is to develop a strategy, or policy, that maximizes its long-term rewards.

Key Concepts in Reinforcement Learning

1. **Agent and Environment**

   - **Agent**: The decision-maker or learner (e.g., a robot, software agent, or character in a game).

   - **Environment**: The external system with which the agent interacts (e.g., a gridworld, game board, or physical space).

2. **State (SSS)**

   - A representation of the environment at a specific point in time.

   - Example: The position of a robot in a warehouse.

3. **Action (AAA)**

   - A decision the agent makes to transition to a new state.

   - Example: Moving left, right, up, or down in a grid.

4. **Reward (RRR)**

   o A scalar value that provides feedback to the agent based on its action.

   o Example: A robot receives +10 for reaching a goal and -1 for hitting an obstacle.

5. **Policy (π\piπ)**

   o A strategy that maps states to actions.

   o Deterministic: Always chooses the same action for a given state.

   o Stochastic: Provides a probability distribution over possible actions.

6. **Value Function (V(s)V(s)V(s))**

   o Estimates the expected cumulative reward an agent will receive starting from state sss.

7. **Q-Value (Action-Value) Function (Q(s,a)Q(s, a)Q(s,a))**

   o Estimates the expected cumulative reward of taking action aaa in state sss.

The RL Learning Process

Reinforcement Learning typically follows these steps:

1. **Observation**: The agent observes the current state (StS_tSt) of the environment.

2. **Action**: The agent selects an action (AtA_tAt) based on its policy.

3. **Transition**: The environment transitions to a new state (St+1S_{t+1}St+1) based on the action.

4. **Reward**: The agent receives a reward (RtR_tRt) for its action.

5. **Update**: The agent updates its policy or value estimates based on the observed reward and state transition.

This process continues iteratively until the agent converges to an optimal policy.

Key Algorithms in Reinforcement Learning

Reinforcement Learning algorithms can be broadly categorized into **value-based methods** and **policy-**

based methods. Let's explore two foundational algorithms: Q-learning and policy gradients.

---

1. Q-Learning

What is Q-Learning?

Q-learning is a value-based RL algorithm that seeks to learn the optimal action-value function, $Q*(s,a)Q^**(s, a)Q*(s,a)$, which represents the maximum expected cumulative reward the agent can achieve starting from state sss and taking action aaa.

The Q-Learning Equation

The Q-value is updated iteratively using the Bellman Equation:

$Q(s,a) \leftarrow Q(s,a)+\alpha[R+\gamma max$⃞$a'Q(s',a')-Q(s,a)]Q(s, a) \leftarrow Q(s, a) + \alpha \left[R + \gamma \max_{a'} Q(s', a') - Q(s, a) \right]Q(s,a) \leftarrow Q(s,a)+\alpha[R+\gamma a' max Q(s',a')-Q(s,a)]$

Where:

- sss: Current state

- aaa: Action taken

- RRR: Reward received

- s's's': New state after taking action aaa

- α\alphaα: Learning rate (controls how much new information overrides old estimates)

- γ\gammaγ: Discount factor (balances immediate and future rewards)

How Q-Learning Works

1. Initialize Q(s,a)Q(s, a)Q(s,a) arbitrarily (often to zero).

2. For each episode:

   o Start in an initial state sss.

   o Choose an action aaa using an exploration strategy (e.g., ϵ\epsilonϵ-greedy).

   o Observe the reward RRR and next state s's's'.

   o Update Q(s,a)Q(s, a)Q(s,a) using the Q-learning equation.

3. Repeat until convergence.

Strengths of Q-Learning

- Model-free: Does not require knowledge of the environment's dynamics.

- Proven to converge to the optimal policy under certain conditions.

Limitations of Q-Learning

- Struggles with large or continuous state spaces.

- Requires a good balance between exploration and exploitation.

---

2. Policy Gradients

What are Policy Gradients?

Policy gradient methods directly optimize the agent's policy (π\pi$\pi$) by maximizing the expected cumulative reward. Unlike Q-learning, which relies on value functions, policy gradients work by parameterizing the policy and updating its parameters.

The Policy Gradient Equation

The policy is updated using the gradient of the objective function:

$\theta \leftarrow \theta + \alpha \nabla_\theta J(\theta)$\theta \leftarrow \theta + \alpha \nabla_\theta J(\theta)$\theta \leftarrow \theta + \alpha \nabla_\theta J(\theta)$

Where:

- θ\theta$\theta$: Parameters of the policy

- $J(\theta)$J(\theta)$J(\theta)$: Objective function (expected cumulative reward)

- α\alpha$\alpha$: Learning rate

How Policy Gradients Work

1. Initialize the policy parameters (θ\theta$\theta$) randomly.

2. Generate episodes by interacting with the environment using the current policy.

3. Compute the gradients of the policy's performance.

4. Update the policy parameters in the direction of the gradient.

5. Repeat until convergence.

Strengths of Policy Gradients

- Suitable for high-dimensional or continuous action spaces.

- Can learn stochastic policies, useful for exploration.

Limitations of Policy Gradients

- High variance in gradient estimates can slow convergence.

- Sensitive to hyperparameters like learning rate.

Advanced Variants

1. **REINFORCE Algorithm**: A simple policy gradient algorithm.

2. **Actor-Critic Methods**: Combine value-based and policy-based approaches to improve efficiency.

Applications of Reinforcement Learning

Reinforcement Learning is revolutionizing industries with its ability to solve complex, sequential decision-making problems. Here are three key domains where RL shines.

1. Robotics

Overview

Robots operate in dynamic environments, making RL an ideal approach for enabling them to learn complex tasks through trial and error.

Applications

- **Manipulation**: Training robotic arms to pick and place objects in manufacturing.

- **Locomotion**: Teaching robots to walk, run, or navigate uneven terrains.

- **Human-Robot Interaction**: Enabling robots to collaborate with humans safely and efficiently.

Example

Boston Dynamics uses RL to train robots like Spot and Atlas for agile locomotion and complex maneuvers.

---

2. Gaming

Overview

Reinforcement Learning has made headlines in the gaming industry by achieving superhuman performance in complex games. Games provide structured environments, making them perfect testbeds for RL research.

Applications

- **Board Games**: AlphaGo used RL to defeat human world champions in Go.

- **Video Games**: RL agents trained with Deep Q-Networks (DQN) can play Atari games with expert-level performance.

- **Multiplayer Games**: OpenAI's Dota 2 bot demonstrated RL's potential in strategic, team-based games.

Example

DeepMind's AlphaZero, an RL-based system, mastered Chess, Shogi, and Go by self-play without prior human knowledge.

---

3. Resource Optimization

Overview

RL excels in optimizing complex systems with competing objectives and dynamic constraints.

Applications

- **Energy Management**: Optimize power grids to balance supply and demand efficiently.

- **Traffic Control**: Reduce congestion by optimizing traffic signals in real time.

- **Inventory Management**: Automate warehouse stocking and supply chain logistics.

Example

Google used RL to optimize energy usage in its data centers, reducing cooling costs by 40%.

Challenges and Future Directions

While RL has demonstrated remarkable success, it also faces challenges:

1. **Exploration vs. Exploitation**: Balancing exploration of new strategies and exploitation of known rewards remains difficult.

2. **Sample Efficiency**: RL often requires large amounts of training data, which can be costly in real-world applications.

3. **Transfer Learning**: Adapting an RL agent trained in one environment to perform well in a new environment is still an open problem.

Future advancements in model-based RL, multi-agent systems, and explainability promise to unlock even more potential for RL in the years ahead.

Reinforcement Learning represents a paradigm shift in machine learning, enabling agents to make decisions and improve through interaction with their environment. By understanding key concepts like reward-based learning, mastering foundational algorithms such as Q-learning and policy gradients, and exploring practical applications in robotics, gaming, and resource optimization, you gain insights into how RL is shaping the future. While challenges remain, RL's ability to tackle complex, real-world problems makes it one of the most exciting areas of AI research and application.

Chapter 13: AI Tools and Frameworks

The field of Artificial Intelligence (AI) is vast and rapidly evolving, but the tools and frameworks available today have made it more accessible than ever before. Whether you are building a simple machine learning model, developing a deep learning system, or managing an entire AI pipeline, the right tools can significantly enhance productivity, accuracy, and collaboration. This chapter provides a comprehensive overview of popular machine learning frameworks, tools for data preprocessing and visualization, and platforms for experiment tracking and collaboration. By understanding these tools, you can streamline your AI workflows and focus on solving real-world problems.

Overview of Popular ML Frameworks: Scikit-learn, TensorFlow, and PyTorch

Modern machine learning frameworks are designed to simplify the development, training, and deployment of AI models. They provide pre-built modules, abstraction layers, and hardware optimization to accelerate workflows while ensuring flexibility and scalability.

1. Scikit-learn

Overview

Scikit-learn is a Python library built on top of NumPy, SciPy, and Matplotlib. It is one of the most popular frameworks for implementing traditional machine learning algorithms. Scikit-learn excels at handling small to medium-sized datasets and provides tools for supervised and unsupervised learning, as well as preprocessing, evaluation, and model selection.

Key Features

1. **Machine Learning Algorithms**:
   - Includes algorithms like linear regression, decision trees, support vector machines, and clustering techniques such as K-means.

2. **Data Preprocessing**:
   - Provides tools for scaling, encoding, imputation, and feature selection.

3. **Model Evaluation**:

   o Supports cross-validation, grid search, and metrics like accuracy, precision, and recall.

4. **Pipeline Integration**:

   o Allows chaining preprocessing steps and model training into a single workflow.

Example: Building a simple regression model in Scikit-learn

python

```
from sklearn.model_selection import train_test_split

from sklearn.linear_model import LinearRegression

from sklearn.metrics import mean_squared_error


# Example dataset

X_train, X_test, y_train, y_test = train_test_split(X, y, test_size=0.2)


# Initialize and train the model
```

```
model = LinearRegression()
model.fit(X_train, y_train)

# Make predictions and evaluate
predictions = model.predict(X_test)
mse = mean_squared_error(y_test, predictions)
print("Mean Squared Error:", mse)
```

Strengths

- User-friendly and well-documented.
- Great for beginners and small-scale projects.

Limitations

- Not designed for deep learning or large-scale distributed systems.

---

2. TensorFlow

Overview

TensorFlow, developed by Google Brain, is a powerful deep learning framework for building, training, and deploying machine learning models. It is widely used for creating neural networks and scaling complex AI systems. TensorFlow supports both low-level API (for customization) and high-level APIs like Keras (for simplicity).

Key Features

1. **Deep Learning Support**:

   o Efficiently handles convolutional neural networks (CNNs), recurrent neural networks (RNNs), and transformers.

2. **Hardware Optimization**:

   o Supports GPU and TPU acceleration for faster training and inference.

3. **TensorFlow Lite**:

   o Facilitates deploying models on mobile and edge devices.

4. **TensorFlow Extended (TFX)**:

   o Provides tools for production-grade model deployment, monitoring, and maintenance.

Example: Building a neural network using TensorFlow

python

```
import tensorflow as tf
```

```python
# Create a Sequential model
model = tf.keras.Sequential([
    tf.keras.layers.Dense(128, activation='relu'),
    tf.keras.layers.Dense(64, activation='relu'),
    tf.keras.layers.Dense(1, activation='sigmoid')
])


# Compile the model
model.compile(optimizer='adam',
loss='binary_crossentropy', metrics=['accuracy'])


# Train the model
model.fit(X_train, y_train, epochs=10,
batch_size=32)
```

Strengths

- Highly scalable and production-ready.
- Extensive community support and a rich ecosystem of tools.

Limitations

- Steeper learning curve for beginners compared to high-level libraries.

---

3. PyTorch

Overview

PyTorch, developed by Facebook's AI Research lab, is another leading deep learning framework. It is known for its dynamic computation graph, which allows greater flexibility and ease of debugging. PyTorch is widely used in academic research and by organizations for cutting-edge AI development.

Key Features

1. **Dynamic Computation Graph**:
   - Unlike TensorFlow's static graphs, PyTorch constructs graphs on the fly, making it intuitive for developers.

2. **Support for Advanced Models**:
   - Includes tools for creating models like GANs (Generative Adversarial Networks) and reinforcement learning agents.

3. **TorchScript**:
   - Converts PyTorch models into a deployable format.

4. **Integration with NumPy:**

    o Seamless interoperability with NumPy for data manipulation.

Example: Building a neural network using PyTorch

python

```python
import torch

import torch.nn as nn

import torch.optim as optim


# Define a simple model
class NeuralNet(nn.Module):
    def __init__(self):
        super(NeuralNet, self).__init__()
        self.fc1 = nn.Linear(64, 128)
        self.fc2 = nn.Linear(128, 1)

    def forward(self, x):
        x = torch.relu(self.fc1(x))
        x = torch.sigmoid(self.fc2(x))
```

```
    return x


# Initialize the model, loss function, and optimizer

model = NeuralNet()

criterion = nn.BCELoss()

optimizer = optim.Adam(model.parameters(),
lr=0.001)


# Training loop

for epoch in range(epochs):

    optimizer.zero_grad()

    outputs = model(X_train)

    loss = criterion(outputs, y_train)

    loss.backward()

    optimizer.step()
```

Strengths

- Intuitive and flexible for researchers.
- Excellent debugging capabilities due to dynamic graphs.

Limitations

- Slightly less production-focused compared to TensorFlow.

Tools for Data Preprocessing and Visualization

The success of machine learning depends heavily on clean, well-prepared data. Tools for preprocessing and visualization play a vital role in exploring data, identifying patterns, and preparing datasets for modeling.

---

1. Data Preprocessing Tools

Pandas

- A Python library for data manipulation and analysis.

- Provides tools for handling missing data, filtering, grouping, and transforming datasets.

NumPy

- Enables efficient numerical computations and manipulation of multi-dimensional arrays.

- Frequently used for feature scaling, matrix operations, and numerical transformations.

OpenCV

- A library for computer vision tasks and image preprocessing.

- Useful for resizing, filtering, and augmenting images in computer vision pipelines.

NLTK and SpaCy

- Libraries for preprocessing textual data.

- Features include tokenization, stemming, lemmatization, and stopword removal for NLP tasks.

---

2. Data Visualization Tools

Matplotlib

- A Python plotting library for creating static, interactive, and publication-quality visualizations.

Seaborn

- Built on top of Matplotlib, it simplifies the creation of statistical visualizations like histograms, heatmaps, and boxplots.

Plotly

- A powerful library for creating interactive visualizations, including 3D plots and dashboards.

Tableau

- A popular tool for creating interactive, shareable dashboards for business intelligence and data visualization.

Example: Plotting a heatmap with Seaborn

python

```
import seaborn as sns
import matplotlib.pyplot as plt

# Example correlation matrix
correlation_matrix = df.corr()

# Heatmap
sns.heatmap(correlation_matrix, annot=True, cmap='coolwarm')
plt.show()
```

Experiment Tracking and Collaboration Tools

Machine learning workflows often involve numerous experiments with different datasets, hyperparameters, and models. Experiment tracking and collaboration tools help manage this complexity while ensuring reproducibility.

---

1. Experiment Tracking Tools

MLflow

- Tracks experiments, records metrics, and saves models for future use.

- Integrates seamlessly with frameworks like TensorFlow and PyTorch.

Weights & Biases (W&B)

- A comprehensive platform for experiment tracking, hyperparameter tuning, and collaboration.

- Features visual dashboards to compare experiments in real time.

Comet.ml

- Tracks experiments and integrates with tools like Scikit-learn and PyTorch.

- Provides insights into hyperparameters, metrics, and model performance.

---

2. Collaboration Tools

Jupyter Notebooks

- An interactive development environment for creating and sharing documents that combine code, visualizations, and narrative text.

Git and GitHub

- Tools for version control and collaboration in machine learning projects.
- Essential for managing codebases and working in teams.

Google Colab

- A cloud-based platform for running Jupyter notebooks with free GPU support.
- Ideal for collaborative experimentation and sharing.

Example: Using MLflow for Experiment Tracking

python

```python
import mlflow

# Start an experiment
mlflow.start_run()

# Log parameters and metrics
mlflow.log_param("learning_rate", 0.01)
mlflow.log_metric("accuracy", 0.85)

# End the experiment
mlflow.end_run()
```

AI tools and frameworks are the backbone of modern machine learning workflows. From Scikit-learn's simplicity in traditional algorithms to TensorFlow and PyTorch's deep learning prowess, these frameworks empower developers and researchers to tackle a wide range of challenges.

Tools for data preprocessing and visualization ensure clean, interpretable data, while experiment tracking platforms like MLflow and W&B enable efficient collaboration and reproducibility. By leveraging these tools, you can enhance productivity, focus on innovation, and build AI solutions that deliver real-world impact.

Chapter 14: Cloud Services for Machine Learning

The rise of cloud computing has revolutionized how machine learning (ML) projects are developed, trained, and deployed. By offering scalable infrastructure, pre-built tools, and managed services, cloud platforms enable organizations and individuals to build powerful ML solutions without investing heavily in on-premise hardware or maintaining complex infrastructure. This chapter explores the benefits of cloud-based ML, provides an overview of leading cloud platforms—AWS SageMaker, Google AI Platform, and Azure Machine Learning—and explains how to deploy ML models in the cloud.

Benefits of Cloud-Based Machine Learning

Cloud services provide an ecosystem of tools and resources designed to streamline every stage of the

ML lifecycle, from data preparation to model deployment. Their advantages make them indispensable for modern ML workflows.

---

1. Scalability and Flexibility

Cloud platforms allow ML projects to scale seamlessly based on workload demands. Whether you're training a small model or processing terabytes of data for deep learning, cloud services dynamically allocate resources as needed.

- **Horizontal Scaling**: Add more virtual machines or instances to handle increased workloads.

- **Vertical Scaling**: Use more powerful computing resources, such as GPUs or TPUs, for faster training.

---

2. Cost Efficiency

Cloud services operate on a pay-as-you-go model, meaning you only pay for the resources you use. This eliminates the upfront capital expenditure of purchasing high-performance hardware.

- **Cost Reduction**: Avoid the need for expensive GPUs, storage, and server maintenance.

- **Optimized Pricing Models**: Choose on-demand, reserved, or spot instances based on budget and workload.

3. Managed Services

Cloud platforms handle much of the complexity associated with setting up and managing ML infrastructure. Managed services abstract away tasks like server configuration, environment setup, and resource allocation, allowing data scientists and developers to focus on building models.

- **No Infrastructure Overhead**: Offload hardware and software management to the cloud provider.

- **Pre-Built Pipelines**: Utilize tools for data preprocessing, feature engineering, and model monitoring.

4. Access to Advanced Tools and Frameworks

Cloud platforms integrate seamlessly with popular ML frameworks like TensorFlow, PyTorch, and Scikit-learn. They also provide cutting-edge tools for AutoML, visualization, and hyperparameter tuning.

- **Pre-Trained Models**: Use APIs for tasks like image recognition, natural language processing, and speech synthesis.

- **Custom Model Training**: Train models from scratch using your own data.

---

5. Global Availability and Collaboration

Cloud platforms are accessible worldwide, enabling teams to collaborate effectively. Features like shared workspaces, version control, and experiment tracking ensure seamless teamwork.

- **Collaboration Tools**: Share notebooks, pipelines, and results with team members.

- **Data Localization**: Deploy applications closer to users for reduced latency.

---

6. Security and Compliance

Cloud providers adhere to strict security protocols, ensuring that data and models are protected. They offer features like encryption, access control, and compliance certifications.

- **Data Encryption**: Protect sensitive data during transit and at rest.

- **Regulatory Compliance**: Meet industry standards like GDPR, HIPAA, and SOC 2.

Overview of Leading Cloud Platforms

The three dominant players in the cloud ML space—AWS SageMaker, Google AI Platform, and Azure Machine Learning—offer robust services for building and deploying ML solutions. Let's explore each platform in detail.

1. AWS SageMaker

Overview

Amazon SageMaker is a fully managed service designed to simplify the ML lifecycle. It provides tools for data preparation, model training, deployment, and monitoring, all integrated into the AWS ecosystem.

Key Features

1. **Built-In Algorithms**:

   o   Pre-built algorithms for tasks like classification, clustering, and anomaly detection.

   o   Example: Linear Learner, XGBoost, and BlazingText.

2. **Notebook Instances**:

   o   Jupyter notebooks preconfigured with popular libraries and frameworks.

3. **AutoML (SageMaker Autopilot)**:

   o   Automatically preprocesses data, trains multiple models, and identifies the best-performing one.

4. **Distributed Training**:

   o   Supports distributed training across multiple GPUs or instances.

5. **Model Deployment and Monitoring**:

   o   Deploy models as REST APIs with auto-scaling and built-in monitoring.

Use Case Example:

A healthcare organization uses SageMaker to predict patient readmission rates by training a model with historical data. The model is deployed as an API, integrating seamlessly with their patient management system.

2. Google AI Platform

Overview

Google AI Platform offers a comprehensive suite of tools for ML workflows, tightly integrated with Google Cloud services. It is particularly strong in AutoML and deep learning due to Google's expertise in AI research.

Key Features

1. **AutoML:**

   o Automates model building for structured data, images, text, and video.

2. **Deep Learning Support:**

   o Native support for TensorFlow, PyTorch, and Keras.

3. **Vertex AI**:

   o A unified platform for managing datasets, training models, and deploying solutions.

4. **TPU Acceleration**:

   o Leverage Tensor Processing Units (TPUs) for ultra-fast training.

5. **Data Integration**:

   o Easily connect to BigQuery, Google Cloud Storage, and other services for data pipelines.

Use Case Example:

An e-commerce company uses Google AI Platform to create personalized product recommendations. With AutoML, they build a deep learning model trained on customer browsing and purchase history.

---

3. Azure Machine Learning (Azure ML)

Overview

Microsoft's Azure Machine Learning is a cloud-based platform for building, deploying, and managing ML models. It emphasizes enterprise-grade features like governance, compliance, and integration with Microsoft tools.

Key Features

1. **Drag-and-Drop Designer**:
   - Build ML pipelines visually without extensive coding.

2. **ML Studio Notebooks**:
   - Jupyter notebooks preloaded with Azure SDKs and ML libraries.

3. **Integration with Azure Services**:
   - Seamless connectivity with Azure Blob Storage, SQL Database, and Power BI.

4. **MLOps**:
   - Tools for CI/CD pipelines, model versioning, and monitoring.

5. **Explainable AI**:
   - Provides insights into model predictions to ensure transparency and trust.

Use Case Example:

A manufacturing firm uses Azure ML to predict equipment failures. The model is deployed into their IoT ecosystem, triggering alerts when anomalies are detected.

Deploying Machine Learning Models in the Cloud

Deploying ML models in the cloud allows businesses to deliver AI solutions at scale, with high availability and low latency. The deployment process involves packaging models, hosting them as APIs, and monitoring their performance.

Steps for Cloud Deployment

1. Prepare the Model

- Train and evaluate the model locally or in the cloud.

- Serialize the model into a format like **ONNX**, **TensorFlow SavedModel**, or **Pickle**.

2. Choose a Deployment Strategy

1. **Batch Predictions**:

   o Process large datasets offline.

   o Example: Predicting churn for all customers in a database.

2. **Real-Time Predictions**:

   o Serve predictions via REST APIs for real-time use cases.

   o Example: Fraud detection during a transaction.

---

3. Containerize the Model

- Use tools like Docker to package the model and its dependencies.

- Example:

dockerfile

FROM python:3.9

COPY model.pkl /app/model.pkl

RUN pip install flask pandas

```
CMD ["python", "app.py"]
```

4. Deploy the Model

1. AWS SageMaker

- o Create an endpoint using SageMaker's deployment tools.

2. Google AI Platform

- o Deploy the model to Vertex AI or a Google Kubernetes Engine (GKE) cluster.

3. Azure ML

- o Use Azure Kubernetes Service (AKS) or Azure Container Instances (ACI) for deployment.

5. Monitor and Maintain

- Use built-in tools for tracking performance, latency, and error rates.

- Enable auto-scaling to handle fluctuating traffic.

Example: Deploying a Model with Flask on AWS

    1. **Set Up Flask API:**

python

```python
from flask import Flask, request, jsonify
import pickle


app = Flask(__name__)
model = pickle.load(open('model.pkl', 'rb'))


@app.route('/predict', methods=['POST'])
def predict():
    data = request.get_json()
    prediction = model.predict([data['features']])
    return jsonify({'prediction': prediction.tolist()})
```

    2. **Containerize and Deploy on AWS Elastic Beanstalk.**

Cloud services have democratized machine learning, enabling individuals and businesses to build scalable, cost-effective, and high-performance AI solutions. Platforms like AWS SageMaker, Google AI Platform, and Azure Machine Learning provide end-to-end tools for every stage of the ML pipeline, from data preparation to model deployment. By leveraging the benefits of cloud-based ML, such as scalability, cost efficiency, and advanced tools, you can focus on solving complex problems while leaving infrastructure management to the experts. Deploying models in the cloud ensures that your AI solutions are robust, accessible, and ready to meet real-world demands.

Chapter 15: Ethics and Bias in AI

As Artificial Intelligence (AI) becomes increasingly embedded in our lives, the importance of ethical considerations in its development and deployment cannot be overstated. While AI has the potential to transform industries and solve complex problems, it also carries the risk of reinforcing biases, violating privacy, and causing unintended harm. Ensuring ethical and responsible AI practices is crucial for building trust, reducing harm, and promoting fairness. This chapter explores the importance of ethics in AI, strategies to identify and mitigate bias in datasets and algorithms, and actionable steps for fostering responsible AI practices.

The Importance of Ethical Considerations

Ethics in AI refers to the principles and guidelines that govern the development, deployment, and use of AI systems to ensure fairness, accountability, transparency, and respect for human rights.

Ignoring ethical considerations can lead to significant societal and legal consequences, including loss of trust, discrimination, and harm to vulnerable populations.

1. Ensuring Fairness and Equity

AI systems often make decisions that directly impact people's lives, such as hiring, loan approvals, and law enforcement. Ethical AI ensures these decisions are fair and equitable, avoiding discrimination based on gender, race, age, or other protected attributes.

Example:

In hiring, biased algorithms trained on historical data may favor male candidates over equally qualified female candidates due to existing gender disparities in past hiring practices. Ensuring fairness in AI models can mitigate such biases and promote inclusivity.

2. Protecting Privacy and Data Security

AI systems rely heavily on data, often collected from individuals. Ethical AI prioritizes the protection of sensitive data, ensuring that privacy is respected and data is used responsibly.

Example:

A facial recognition system collecting data without explicit consent raises privacy concerns, potentially violating regulations like GDPR or CCPA.

---

3. Preventing Harm

AI systems, if poorly designed, can cause significant harm. Ethical considerations aim to minimize unintended consequences and ensure that AI benefits humanity without exacerbating existing problems.

Example:

Autonomous vehicles rely on AI to make split-second decisions. A lack of ethical oversight in their programming could lead to decisions that prioritize property over human lives.

---

4. Building Trust in AI Systems

Public trust is essential for the widespread adoption of AI. Transparent and ethical AI practices foster trust among users, stakeholders, and society at large.

Example:

Explainable AI models that provide clear reasoning behind their predictions (e.g., why a loan was approved or denied) can increase trust and acceptance among users.

Identifying and Mitigating Bias in Datasets and Algorithms

Bias in AI arises when an algorithm produces prejudiced outcomes due to biased data, flawed design, or inappropriate training methods. Addressing bias is a critical component of ethical AI development.

---

1. Types of Bias in AI

1.1 Data Bias

- Occurs when the training data used to build the model is unrepresentative or contains historical prejudices.

- **Example**: A facial recognition system trained primarily on lighter-skinned faces may perform poorly on darker-skinned individuals.

1.2 Algorithmic Bias

- Arises from the design of the algorithm itself, including how features are weighted or prioritized.

- **Example**: A hiring algorithm that overly prioritizes technical skills might unintentionally disadvantage candidates from diverse educational backgrounds.

1.3 Interaction Bias

- Results from user interactions with the AI system.

- **Example**: Search engines showing biased results based on common user queries.

---

2. Steps to Identify Bias

2.1 Audit Data

- Examine the dataset for imbalances, missing values, or overrepresentation of certain groups.

- **Example**: Check whether demographic groups are proportionally represented in a training dataset.

2.2 Analyze Model Outputs

- Evaluate predictions across different groups to identify disparities.

- **Example**: Compare the accuracy of a predictive model for different genders or ethnicities.

2.3 Use Fairness Metrics

- Employ metrics to measure bias, such as:

  - **Demographic Parity**: Ensures equal treatment across groups.

  - **Equalized Odds**: Compares false positive and false negative rates across groups.

---

3. Strategies to Mitigate Bias

3.1 Preprocessing Data

- Balance the dataset by oversampling underrepresented groups or undersampling overrepresented ones.

- Remove sensitive attributes (e.g., race, gender) from the training data when appropriate.

3.2 Algorithmic Fairness

- Use fairness-aware algorithms that explicitly account for equity during training.

- Regularize models to penalize biased outcomes.

3.3 Post-Processing

- Adjust model predictions after training to ensure fairness.

- **Example:** Calibrate probabilities to achieve equal accuracy across groups.

3.4 Diversify Teams

- Include individuals from diverse backgrounds in the development process to bring varied perspectives and reduce blind spots.

Responsible AI Practices

Responsible AI goes beyond addressing bias to encompass principles like accountability, transparency, and societal impact. Implementing responsible AI practices ensures that AI systems align with ethical values and legal frameworks.

1. Accountability

Why It Matters

Accountability ensures that individuals and organizations take responsibility for the outcomes of their AI systems, whether intended or unintended.

Best Practices

- Clearly define roles and responsibilities for AI development and deployment.

- Maintain a clear audit trail for decisions made by AI systems.

- Establish a governance framework to oversee ethical AI practices.

2. Transparency and Explainability

Why It Matters

Transparent AI systems help users understand how decisions are made, fostering trust and enabling accountability.

Best Practices

- Use interpretable models where possible, such as decision trees or linear regression.

- For complex models (e.g., deep learning), employ explainability techniques like SHAP (Shapley Additive Explanations) to provide insights into predictions.

---

3. Inclusivity

Why It Matters

Inclusive AI systems avoid marginalizing specific groups and promote equitable outcomes.

Best Practices

- Engage stakeholders from diverse demographics during model design and testing.

- Regularly evaluate models to ensure they remain unbiased as societal norms evolve.

---

4. Adherence to Ethical Frameworks

Organizations and researchers should adhere to established ethical frameworks to guide their AI practices.

Examples of Ethical Frameworks

1. **AI Ethics Guidelines by the EU**: Emphasizes fairness, accountability, and transparency.

2. **IEEE Ethically Aligned Design**: Provides standards for ethical AI system design.

3. **Principles of Asilomar AI**: Focuses on long-term societal impacts and safety.

---

5. Continuous Monitoring and Feedback

Why It Matters

AI systems can degrade over time as data distributions shift. Continuous monitoring ensures they remain reliable and fair.

Best Practices

- Regularly retrain models on updated data.

- Monitor performance metrics for signs of bias or degradation.

- Solicit user feedback to identify potential issues.

Case Studies and Real-World Examples

1. Bias in Recruitment Algorithms

A major corporation deployed an AI recruitment tool to screen resumes. The tool disproportionately favored male candidates because it was trained on historical data where men were overrepresented in senior roles. The company mitigated this by retraining the model on a balanced dataset and removing gender-specific attributes.

2. Facial Recognition and Racial Bias

Studies revealed that some facial recognition systems had higher error rates for darker-skinned individuals. Companies responded by improving dataset diversity and implementing fairness constraints in model training.

3. Autonomous Vehicles and Ethical Dilemmas

Autonomous vehicles face ethical dilemmas in crash scenarios, such as prioritizing passenger safety over pedestrian safety. Developers addressed this by involving ethicists and policymakers in the decision-making process to define acceptable trade-offs.

Ethics and bias in AI are not just technical challenges but societal imperatives. By prioritizing fairness, transparency, and accountability, we can harness AI's transformative potential while minimizing harm and fostering trust. Identifying and mitigating bias in datasets and algorithms is essential for building equitable systems. Responsible AI practices—encompassing inclusivity, monitoring, and adherence to ethical frameworks—ensure that AI benefits all of humanity. As developers, researchers, and organizations, it is our collective responsibility to create AI that is not only intelligent but also just and humane.

Chapter 16: Scaling Machine Learning Models

As machine learning (ML) models evolve to tackle increasingly complex problems, the demand for scalability becomes critical. Whether working with massive datasets, training deep learning models, or deploying solutions to handle high traffic, scaling ML systems is a core challenge. Successfully scaling ML models requires addressing bottlenecks in computation, storage, and deployment, and leveraging distributed systems and parallelization. This chapter explores the challenges in scaling ML solutions, delves into distributed training and model parallelism, and examines tools like Apache Spark and Dask that empower developers to build scalable, efficient ML workflows.

Challenges in Scaling ML Solutions

Scaling ML models is not as simple as adding more compute power or storage. It involves addressing multiple technical and operational challenges that arise when transitioning from small-scale experiments to production-grade systems.

1. Computational Complexity

The Problem

As datasets grow larger and models become more complex, the computational demands increase exponentially. Training deep learning models with millions of parameters on large datasets can take days or even weeks on standard hardware.

Impact

- Increased training times delay iterations and experimentation.

- High computational requirements may exceed the capabilities of traditional single-machine setups.

2. Memory and Storage Limitations

The Problem

Large datasets and model parameters often exceed the memory capacity of a single machine. For example, high-resolution image datasets or text corpora for natural language processing (NLP) can be terabytes in size.

Impact

- Inability to load entire datasets into memory leads to inefficiencies in data processing.

- Model weights and intermediate computations during training may overwhelm available GPU or CPU memory.

---

3. Distributed System Complexity

The Problem

Distributing tasks across multiple machines introduces challenges in synchronization, fault tolerance, and data consistency.

Impact

- Communication overhead can negate the benefits of parallel processing.

- Debugging and maintaining distributed systems is more complex compared to single-node setups.

---

4. Data Management

The Problem

Preprocessing and feeding large datasets into ML models efficiently is critical. Poor data management can create bottlenecks in I/O operations, limiting overall system performance.

Impact

- Slow data pipelines delay training and inference.

- Poorly partitioned or unbalanced data in distributed systems leads to underutilization of resources.

---

5. Deployment Challenges

The Problem

Deploying scalable ML models requires handling fluctuating traffic, ensuring low-latency predictions, and maintaining reliability across distributed systems.

Impact

- Systems may fail to scale dynamically to accommodate high-demand periods.

- Latency and availability issues degrade user experience.

Distributed Training and Model Parallelism

Scaling ML models often involves distributing the workload across multiple CPUs, GPUs, or machines. Two primary approaches—**data parallelism** and **model parallelism**—are used to achieve this.

---

1. Data Parallelism

What is Data Parallelism?

In data parallelism, the dataset is divided into smaller batches, and each batch is processed independently on separate machines or devices. The model remains the same on all nodes.

How It Works

1. Each device receives a subset of the data.

2. The model computes gradients locally for its assigned data.

3. Gradients from all devices are aggregated and averaged.

4. Model weights are updated based on the averaged gradients.

Strengths

- Scales efficiently with large datasets.

- Easy to implement using modern frameworks like TensorFlow and PyTorch.

Challenges

- Communication overhead during gradient aggregation.

- Requires synchronized updates, which can cause delays.

---

2. Model Parallelism

What is Model Parallelism?

In model parallelism, the model itself is divided across multiple devices. Each device is responsible for computing a subset of the model's layers or operations.

How It Works

1. Model layers are split across devices.

2. Data flows sequentially through devices, with each device computing its assigned layers.

3. Gradients are computed and backpropagated across devices.

Strengths

- Ideal for extremely large models that cannot fit into the memory of a single device.

- Reduces memory bottlenecks.

Challenges

- Sequential data flow can introduce latency.

- Complex to implement and debug.

3. Hybrid Parallelism

Hybrid parallelism combines data and model parallelism to optimize resource utilization. This approach is particularly effective for large-scale systems requiring both extensive datasets and complex models.

Distributed Training Frameworks

1. Horovod

- Open-source library for distributed training of deep learning models.

- Built on top of TensorFlow, PyTorch, and Keras.

- Uses ring-allreduce for efficient gradient aggregation.

2. NVIDIA NCCL

- Optimizes communication between GPUs for multi-GPU training.

- Provides high-speed interconnects for data transfer.

Tools for Scaling: Apache Spark and Dask

To overcome the challenges of scaling, developers leverage distributed computing frameworks like Apache Spark and Dask. These tools enable efficient data processing and scalable machine learning workflows.

---

1. Apache Spark

Overview

Apache Spark is a distributed computing platform designed for big data processing. Its MLlib library provides scalable implementations of common machine learning algorithms.

Key Features

1. **In-Memory Computation**

   o Stores intermediate results in
      memory, reducing I/O overhead.

2. **Fault Tolerance**

   o Automatically replicates data and
      tasks, ensuring system resilience.

3. **Distributed Machine Learning (MLlib)**

   o Includes algorithms like linear
      regression, clustering, and
      recommendation systems.

4. **Scalability**

   o Processes terabytes of data across
      distributed nodes.

**Example: Running a Machine Learning Workflow
in Spark**

python

```
from pyspark.ml.classification import
LogisticRegression
```

```python
from pyspark.ml.feature import VectorAssembler

from pyspark.sql import SparkSession


# Initialize Spark session

spark =
SparkSession.builder.appName("MLScaling").getOr
Create()


# Load data

data = spark.read.csv("data.csv", header=True,
inferSchema=True)


# Preprocessing

assembler =
VectorAssembler(inputCols=["feature1",
"feature2"], outputCol="features")

data = assembler.transform(data)


# Train model

lr = LogisticRegression(featuresCol="features",
labelCol="label")

model = lr.fit(data)
```

```
# Make predictions

predictions = model.transform(data)

predictions.show()
```

Strengths

- Handles massive datasets effectively.

- Integrates with Hadoop and other big data tools.

Limitations

- Higher latency compared to frameworks optimized for GPU-based deep learning.

---

2. Dask

Overview

Dask is a Python-based parallel computing library that extends familiar Python tools like Pandas and NumPy for distributed environments.

Key Features

1. **Parallel DataFrames and Arrays**

   o Scales Pandas and NumPy operations to larger-than-memory datasets.

2. **Dynamic Task Scheduling**

   o Automatically schedules and executes tasks across distributed resources.

3. **Integration with ML Libraries**

   o Works seamlessly with Scikit-learn for distributed training.

Example: Scaling Data Preprocessing with Dask

python

```python
import dask.dataframe as dd

# Load data
df = dd.read_csv("large_dataset.csv")

# Preprocessing
df = df[df["column"] > 0]
df["new_column"] = df["column"] * 2

# Compute results
result = df.compute()
```

```
print(result.head())
```

Strengths

- Easy to integrate into existing Python workflows.

- Scales on both single machines and clusters.

Limitations

- Less optimized for deep learning compared to TensorFlow or PyTorch.

Case Study: Scaling an ML Pipeline

Problem

A financial institution needed to build a credit risk model using terabytes of transaction data. The dataset was too large to process on a single machine, and training deep learning models required efficient resource allocation.

Solution

1. **Data Preprocessing with Apache Spark**

   o Used Spark to preprocess the transaction data across a distributed Hadoop cluster.

2. **Model Training with Horovod**

   o Trained a neural network using TensorFlow and Horovod on a GPU cluster.

3. **Deployment with Kubernetes**

   o Deployed the model as a scalable REST API, using Kubernetes to handle traffic spikes.

Outcome

- Reduced data processing time by 80%.

- Achieved real-time inference with minimal latency.

Scaling machine learning models is essential for handling large datasets, complex algorithms, and production-level deployments. By understanding and addressing challenges such as computational complexity, memory limitations, and distributed system intricacies, organizations can build robust and efficient systems. Distributed training techniques like data and model parallelism, combined with tools like Apache Spark and Dask, provide the infrastructure needed to scale ML workflows seamlessly. With these approaches, developers can harness the full potential of ML, delivering impactful solutions at scale.

Chapter 17: MLOps: Machine Learning Operations

As machine learning (ML) models increasingly transition from experimental projects to production systems, the challenges of deploying, monitoring, and maintaining them at scale have come into sharp focus. MLOps, or Machine Learning Operations, has emerged as a discipline that combines best practices from software engineering, data engineering, and machine learning to streamline the ML lifecycle. Similar to DevOps in software development, MLOps focuses on automation, collaboration, and continuous delivery to ensure reliable and scalable ML systems. In this chapter, we'll explore the concept of MLOps and its importance, delve into CI/CD pipelines for ML projects, and examine strategies for monitoring and maintaining deployed models.

The Concept of MLOps and Its Importance

MLOps refers to the practices and tools that help operationalize ML workflows, bridging the gap between model development and deployment. While traditional ML workflows often end with model training, MLOps addresses the complexities of deploying models, managing infrastructure, and ensuring their long-term reliability.

Why MLOps Is Important

1. **Streamlining the ML Lifecycle**

    o The ML lifecycle includes data preprocessing, model training, deployment, and maintenance. MLOps standardizes and automates these stages, reducing friction between teams.

2. **Scalability and Reliability**

    o Models deployed without proper practices often fail to scale or adapt to changing environments. MLOps ensures that models remain reliable even under heavy workloads or when data distributions shift.

3. **Reproducibility**

   o Data scientists frequently face challenges reproducing results due to changing datasets, environments, or code. MLOps enforces version control for data, code, and models, ensuring consistency.

4. **Collaboration Across Teams**

   o MLOps promotes collaboration between data scientists, engineers, and operations teams by defining clear roles and responsibilities.

5. **Faster Iterations**

   o By automating repetitive tasks such as data validation, model testing, and deployment, MLOps allows teams to experiment and iterate more rapidly.

Core Principles of MLOps

1. **Automation**

   o Automate repetitive tasks such as data preprocessing, model training, testing, and deployment to save time and reduce human error.

2. **Continuous Integration and Continuous Deployment (CI/CD)**

   o CI/CD pipelines ensure seamless integration of code changes and rapid deployment of models.

3. **Monitoring and Feedback Loops**

   o Continuously monitor model performance in production and incorporate feedback to retrain models or adjust parameters.

4. **Version Control**

   o Track versions of datasets, models, and code to ensure reproducibility and auditability.

5. **Scalability**

   o Build systems that can handle increasing data volumes and user demands without degrading performance.

CI/CD Pipelines for ML Projects

CI/CD pipelines, a staple of modern software development, are equally crucial in ML projects.

However, ML pipelines are more complex due to the involvement of datasets, model artifacts, and hyperparameter tuning. A well-designed CI/CD pipeline automates the process of testing, building, and deploying ML models, ensuring faster and more reliable delivery.

---

1. Continuous Integration (CI)

Continuous Integration focuses on integrating and testing code changes frequently to identify issues early. In ML projects, CI extends to validating datasets, preprocessing scripts, and model training code.

Key Steps in CI for ML

1. **Code Integration**

    o Use version control systems like Git to track changes in code and manage contributions from multiple developers.

2. **Automated Testing**

    o Write unit tests for preprocessing functions, model evaluation metrics, and training pipelines.

- o Example: Verify that a data preprocessing script handles missing values correctly.

3. **Data Validation**

   - o Ensure datasets meet predefined quality standards using tools like TensorFlow Data Validation.

   - o Example: Check for missing values, duplicates, or anomalies in the dataset.

4. **Model Training Validation**

   - o Run automated tests to confirm that training scripts execute without errors.

   - o Example: Verify that hyperparameter tuning scripts converge within a reasonable time frame.

---

2. Continuous Deployment (CD)

Continuous Deployment automates the release of ML models to production environments, ensuring that new models can be deployed quickly and reliably.

Key Steps in CD for ML

1. **Model Packaging**

    o Serialize the trained model into a deployable format, such as ONNX or TensorFlow SavedModel.

2. **Integration Testing**

    o Test the model with production-like data to ensure compatibility with downstream systems.

3. **Deployment to Production**

    o Use orchestration tools like Kubernetes or AWS SageMaker to deploy the model as a scalable API or batch-processing service.

4. **Rollback Mechanisms**

    o Implement rollback strategies to revert to previous model versions in case of failures.

---

3. Tools for Building CI/CD Pipelines

1. **GitHub Actions**

    o Automate workflows for testing and deploying ML code.

2. **Jenkins**

   o Set up custom CI/CD pipelines with plugins for ML workflows.

3. **Kubeflow Pipelines**

   o Orchestrate end-to-end ML workflows on Kubernetes.

4. **MLflow**

   o Manage the lifecycle of ML models, from tracking experiments to deployment.

Example: CI/CD Pipeline for a Sentiment Analysis Model

1. **Continuous Integration**

   o Run tests for preprocessing scripts to clean text data.

   o Validate that the model achieves a minimum accuracy on validation data.

2. **Continuous Deployment**

   o Package the trained model into a Flask API.

- o Deploy the API to a Kubernetes cluster using CI/CD tools.

Monitoring and Maintaining Deployed Models

Deploying a model is not the end of the ML lifecycle. Continuous monitoring and maintenance are essential to ensure models remain accurate, fair, and reliable in production.

1. The Importance of Monitoring

Models in production are exposed to dynamic environments, where changes in data distributions or user behavior can degrade performance. Monitoring helps detect such issues and triggers corrective actions.

Challenges in Monitoring

- **Data Drift**: Changes in input data distributions compared to training data.

- **Concept Drift**: Changes in the relationship between input features and target labels.

- **Latency**: Increased response times due to inefficient deployment configurations.

2. Monitoring Metrics for ML Models

Model Performance Metrics

- Accuracy, precision, recall, and F1-score for classification models.

- RMSE or MAE for regression models.

Operational Metrics

- Latency: Time taken for the model to return predictions.

- Throughput: Number of predictions processed per second.

Fairness Metrics

- Evaluate disparities in model performance across different demographic groups.

---

3. Tools for Monitoring

1. **Prometheus and Grafana**

   o Monitor system-level metrics like latency, throughput, and resource usage.

2. **Evidently AI**

   o Track model performance metrics and detect data or concept drift.

3. **Seldon Core**

   o Monitor deployed models for predictions and errors in Kubernetes environments.

---

4. Retraining and Updating Models

Continuous monitoring feeds into the retraining and updating phase, ensuring models remain relevant and accurate.

Steps for Retraining

1. **Data Collection**

   o Collect real-world data and label it if necessary.

2. **Error Analysis**

   o Identify patterns in incorrect predictions to refine the model.

3. **Incremental Training**

   o Fine-tune the model using newly collected data without retraining from scratch.

4. **Deployment**

   o Deploy the updated model using the existing CI/CD pipeline.

5. Example: Maintaining a Fraud Detection Model

1. Monitoring

- Track false positive and false negative rates to detect concept drift.
- Use alerts to notify the team if performance drops below a threshold.

2. Retraining

- Incorporate new transaction data with labels into the training dataset.
- Fine-tune the model and validate its performance.

3. Deployment

- Deploy the retrained model using a blue-green deployment strategy to ensure zero downtime.

MLOps is a critical discipline for building, deploying, and maintaining machine learning models at scale. By integrating practices like CI/CD and leveraging monitoring tools, organizations can ensure their ML systems are robust, reliable, and adaptable to changing environments. As ML systems become more complex and ubiquitous, MLOps will continue to play a pivotal role in bridging the gap between experimentation and production, enabling faster innovation and greater business impact.

Chapter 18: Real-World Applications of AI

Artificial Intelligence (AI) is no longer confined to research labs or speculative fiction—it is transforming industries, solving pressing societal challenges, and creating entirely new opportunities. From personalized healthcare to real-time fraud detection and adaptive learning systems, AI applications are reshaping the world as we know it. In this chapter, we'll explore how AI is revolutionizing key sectors like healthcare, finance, and education, examine examples of AI for social good, and discuss emerging trends and innovative applications that hold promise for the future.

AI in Healthcare

The healthcare industry has been one of the most significant beneficiaries of AI advancements, with applications ranging from diagnostics to drug discovery and personalized medicine. AI-powered tools are improving patient outcomes, reducing costs, and addressing inefficiencies in the medical ecosystem.

1. Diagnostics and Medical Imaging

AI excels in processing large amounts of medical data, particularly in imaging, where it often outperforms human experts in detecting abnormalities.

Examples

1. **Radiology**:

    o Deep learning models analyze X-rays, MRIs, and CT scans to detect conditions such as tumors, fractures, or organ anomalies.

    o Example: Google's AI model for breast cancer detection has achieved higher accuracy than radiologists in some studies.

2. **Pathology**:

    o AI algorithms assist in analyzing tissue samples for diseases like cancer.

2. Drug Discovery

The traditional drug discovery process is time-consuming and expensive. AI accelerates this process by analyzing molecular structures, predicting drug interactions, and identifying potential candidates.

Examples

- **Insilico Medicine**: Used AI to identify new drug candidates for fibrosis in less than 18 months.

- **DeepMind's AlphaFold**: Accurately predicts protein folding, a breakthrough for understanding diseases and designing drugs.

---

3. Personalized Medicine

AI enables the development of treatment plans tailored to individual patients by analyzing genetic information, medical history, and lifestyle data.

Examples

- AI-driven tools recommend cancer therapies based on tumor genomics.

- Wearable devices like Fitbit or Apple Watch collect real-time health data, enabling AI algorithms to provide personalized health advice.

---

4. Virtual Health Assistants

AI chatbots and virtual assistants are transforming how patients interact with healthcare providers, offering round-the-clock support for common queries, appointment scheduling, and medication reminders.

Examples

- **Babylon Health**: Provides AI-powered medical consultations via a mobile app.

- **Ada Health**: Uses AI to assess symptoms and guide patients to appropriate care.

Challenges in AI Healthcare Applications

- **Data Privacy**: Ensuring patient confidentiality while using large datasets.

- **Bias**: Avoiding bias in AI models trained on non-representative datasets.

- **Regulation**: Complying with healthcare regulations like HIPAA and GDPR.

AI in Finance

The financial industry has embraced AI to optimize operations, enhance customer experiences, and improve risk management. AI's ability to process massive datasets in real-time makes it invaluable in this sector.

---

1. Fraud Detection

AI systems analyze transaction data to detect unusual patterns or anomalies that may indicate fraudulent activity.

Examples

- Credit card companies use machine learning models to flag potentially fraudulent transactions in real time.

- Banks employ AI systems to detect money laundering through pattern recognition.

---

2. Algorithmic Trading

AI powers high-frequency trading systems that analyze market trends and execute trades at lightning speed, maximizing profits while minimizing risks.

Examples

- AI-based trading platforms like QuantConnect and Alpaca leverage predictive analytics to identify profitable trades.

- Hedge funds like Renaissance Technologies use AI to analyze financial markets and develop trading strategies.

---

3. Personalized Financial Services

AI enables financial institutions to offer personalized services, including investment advice, credit scoring, and customer support.

Examples

- **Robo-Advisors**: Platforms like Betterment and Wealthfront provide automated investment advice tailored to individual risk profiles.

- **Chatbots**: AI-driven assistants like Erica (Bank of America) and Eno (Capital One) help customers manage accounts and budgets.

---

4. Risk Assessment

AI models evaluate credit risk by analyzing an applicant's financial history, reducing manual errors and improving decision-making accuracy.

Examples

- AI-powered credit scoring systems analyze alternative data, such as social media activity and utility payments, to assess creditworthiness.

Challenges in AI Finance Applications

- **Ethics**: Avoiding discrimination in credit scoring algorithms.

- **Cybersecurity**: Protecting sensitive financial data from cyberattacks.

- **Transparency**: Ensuring explainability in AI-driven decisions.

AI in Education

AI is transforming the education sector by personalizing learning experiences, improving administrative efficiency, and making education more accessible worldwide.

---

1. Adaptive Learning Systems

AI-driven platforms customize learning materials and pacing based on individual student needs, helping learners progress at their own speed.

Examples

- **DreamBox Learning**: Uses AI to adapt math lessons for K-12 students.

- **Coursera**: Offers AI-powered recommendations for courses based on a learner's goals and progress.

---

2. Intelligent Tutoring Systems

AI-powered tutors provide real-time feedback and guidance, supplementing classroom instruction or supporting self-paced learners.

Examples

- **Carnegie Learning**: Combines AI with cognitive science to provide personalized math tutoring.

- **Socratic by Google**: Uses AI to answer homework questions and explain concepts.

---

3. Automated Administrative Tasks

AI streamlines administrative functions, such as grading assignments, scheduling classes, and managing enrollment.

Examples

- Automated grading tools for multiple-choice and essay-based assessments.

- AI chatbots handle student inquiries about admission processes or campus resources.

---

4. Bridging Accessibility Gaps

AI technologies make education more inclusive by addressing accessibility challenges for students with disabilities.

Examples

- Speech-to-text tools for hearing-impaired students.

- AI-based translation tools for multilingual classrooms.

Challenges in AI Education Applications

- **Equity**: Ensuring AI tools are accessible to underserved communities.

- **Data Privacy**: Protecting sensitive student information.

- **Teacher-Student Balance**: Avoiding over-reliance on technology at the expense of human interaction.

AI for Social Good: Examples and Case Studies

AI is being used to tackle some of the world's most pressing challenges, from climate change to poverty alleviation and disaster response. These applications demonstrate how AI can serve as a force for social good.

---

1. Disaster Response

AI helps predict and respond to natural disasters by analyzing environmental data and providing real-time updates.

Examples

- **Google AI for Flood Forecasting**: Provides early warnings to communities at risk of flooding.

- **UNICEF's Magic Box**: Uses AI to predict the spread of diseases like Zika during humanitarian crises.

2. Wildlife Conservation

AI-powered tools are used to monitor endangered species, combat poaching, and analyze ecosystems.

Examples

- **Wildbook**: Uses computer vision to identify and track individual animals from photos and videos.

- **PAWS (Protection Assistant for Wildlife Security)**: Optimizes ranger patrol routes using AI to prevent poaching.

3. Fighting Hunger and Poverty

AI is applied to optimize food distribution, monitor crop health, and identify at-risk populations.

Examples

- **World Food Programme**: Uses AI to analyze satellite imagery and predict food shortages.

- **Microsoft AI for Earth**: Supports sustainable agriculture by providing insights into soil health and crop yields.

---

4. Public Health

AI assists in disease surveillance, vaccine distribution, and improving access to healthcare in remote areas.

Examples

- **BlueDot**: Predicted the outbreak of COVID-19 by analyzing airline data and news reports.

- AI-driven mobile health units provide diagnostics in underserved regions.

Emerging Trends and Innovative Applications

As AI technology advances, new trends and applications are emerging that promise to redefine what's possible across industries and societies.

---

1. Generative AI

Generative AI models, such as OpenAI's GPT and DALL·E, are creating new possibilities for content creation, design, and innovation.

Applications

- Generating realistic images, videos, and text for entertainment and marketing.
- Enhancing creativity in fields like fashion, architecture, and graphic design.

---

2. AI in Space Exploration

AI is aiding space exploration by analyzing vast amounts of data collected from telescopes and spacecraft.

Examples

- NASA uses AI to identify exoplanets from Kepler telescope data.

- Autonomous AI systems guide rovers on Mars to navigate terrains and conduct experiments.

---

3. AI and Quantum Computing

The integration of AI with quantum computing holds promise for solving problems that are currently intractable for classical computers.

Potential Applications

- Optimizing supply chains and logistics.

- Accelerating drug discovery through quantum simulations.

---

4. AI for Mental Health

AI-driven apps and chatbots are providing mental health support by offering therapy sessions, mood tracking, and stress management tips.

Examples

- **Woebot**: An AI-powered chatbot that offers cognitive behavioral therapy.

- **Wysa**: Uses AI to provide empathetic conversations and coping strategies.

---

5. Ethical AI and Governance

As AI adoption grows, there is increasing focus on building ethical AI systems that prioritize transparency, fairness, and accountability.

Emerging Practices

- Developing explainable AI models.

- Creating frameworks to govern AI use in sensitive areas like law enforcement and employment.

The real-world applications of AI are vast, spanning industries, geographies, and societal needs. From transforming healthcare and finance to driving social good and fostering innovation, AI is shaping the future in profound ways. However, the responsible and ethical deployment of AI remains critical to ensuring its benefits are equitable and sustainable. As we embrace emerging trends and explore innovative applications, the possibilities for AI to enhance lives and solve global challenges are limitless.

Chapter 19: Challenges in AI Implementation

Implementing Artificial Intelligence (AI) in real-world applications holds immense promise, but it is not without challenges. While AI has the potential to transform industries and solve complex problems, many organizations encounter significant roadblocks when integrating AI into their workflows. These challenges stem from technical, organizational, and societal factors, making AI implementation a multifaceted endeavor. This chapter explores common roadblocks in machine learning (ML) projects, strategies to overcome these challenges, and ways to adapt to the rapidly changing AI landscape.

Common Roadblocks in AI Implementation

Despite the enthusiasm surrounding AI, many projects fail to progress from proof-of-concept to full-scale deployment. These failures often arise from a combination of technical and non-technical obstacles.

---

1. Data-Related Challenges

Data is the cornerstone of AI, and its quality, accessibility, and volume directly influence the success of AI projects. However, data-related issues are among the most significant barriers to AI implementation.

1.1 Data Quality

- **Problem**: Incomplete, inconsistent, or inaccurate data can lead to biased or unreliable AI models.

- **Example**: An AI model trained on incomplete customer data may make incorrect predictions, leading to poor business decisions.

1.2 Data Volume

- **Problem**: Insufficient data may prevent models from learning effectively, while excessive data can strain storage and computational resources.

- **Example**: Small datasets may lead to overfitting, while big datasets can increase training times.

1.3 Data Silos

- **Problem**: Organizations often store data in isolated systems, making it difficult to aggregate and analyze.

- **Example**: A healthcare provider with patient data distributed across multiple departments may struggle to build a comprehensive AI model.

1.4 Regulatory and Privacy Constraints

- **Problem**: Laws like GDPR and HIPAA impose strict regulations on data usage and storage.

- **Example**: An AI system designed for personalized advertising must ensure compliance with privacy laws.

---

2. Talent and Expertise Gaps

The success of AI projects depends on skilled professionals, yet many organizations lack the required expertise.

2.1 Shortage of AI Talent

- **Problem**: Skilled data scientists, ML engineers, and AI researchers are in high demand but short supply.

- **Example**: A company may delay AI implementation due to difficulty hiring experts.

2.2 Training Non-Technical Staff

- **Problem**: Employees unfamiliar with AI may resist its adoption or struggle to integrate it into existing workflows.

- **Example**: A sales team may hesitate to use AI-driven CRM tools without adequate training.

3. Integration with Existing Systems

AI models often need to work alongside legacy systems, which can be difficult to integrate and modernize.

Problem

- Legacy systems may lack APIs or scalable architecture, making it challenging to deploy AI models.

- **Example**: An AI-powered recommendation engine may require real-time data access from an outdated database.

4. Unrealistic Expectations

Overhyped expectations about AI's capabilities often lead to disappointment when real-world results fall short.

Problem

- Stakeholders may expect AI to deliver immediate, perfect results without understanding its limitations.

- **Example**: A company might abandon a predictive maintenance project because the model doesn't achieve 100% accuracy.

5. Cost and Resource Constraints

AI projects can be resource-intensive, requiring significant investments in hardware, software, and talent.

Problem

- Smaller organizations may struggle to afford high-performance GPUs, cloud computing, and expert salaries.

- **Example**: A startup might halt a deep learning project due to budget overruns.

6. Ethical and Bias Concerns

AI systems are prone to biases inherited from training data or flawed design.

Problem

- Biased AI models can perpetuate societal inequalities or produce unfair outcomes.

- **Example:** A hiring algorithm may favor male candidates if trained on biased historical hiring data.

Strategies for Overcoming Challenges

Successfully navigating the complexities of AI implementation requires proactive strategies that address both technical and organizational barriers.

---

1. Addressing Data Challenges

1.1 Data Cleaning and Preprocessing

- Invest in robust data cleaning pipelines to remove inconsistencies, handle missing values, and standardize formats.

- Use tools like Pandas for preprocessing structured data or OpenRefine for cleaning messy datasets.

1.2 Data Augmentation

- Use data augmentation techniques to generate synthetic data and improve model robustness.

- **Example**: Rotate, flip, or crop images to augment datasets for computer vision tasks.

1.3 Breaking Down Silos

- Implement data lakes or warehouses to centralize data from disparate sources.

- Use ETL (Extract, Transform, Load) tools like Apache Nifi or Talend to integrate siloed data.

1.4 Ensuring Compliance

- Employ privacy-preserving techniques such as federated learning or differential privacy.

- Consult legal experts to ensure compliance with data regulations.

2. Bridging the Talent Gap

2.1 Upskilling Existing Staff

- Offer AI and ML training programs for employees to develop in-house expertise.

- Platforms like Coursera, edX, and DataCamp provide accessible learning paths.

2.2 Hiring AI Experts

- Collaborate with academic institutions or AI consultancies to access skilled professionals.

- Offer competitive compensation packages to attract top talent.

2.3 Fostering Cross-Disciplinary Teams

- Create teams that combine technical, domain, and business expertise to ensure AI projects align with organizational goals.

---

3. Integrating with Legacy Systems

3.1 API Development

- Develop APIs or middleware to enable seamless communication between AI models and legacy systems.

- Use frameworks like Flask or FastAPI to deploy AI models as RESTful services.

3.2 Gradual Modernization

- Modernize legacy systems incrementally, starting with components that are most critical to AI integration.

---

4. Managing Expectations

4.1 Educating Stakeholders

- Conduct workshops or presentations to educate stakeholders about AI's capabilities and limitations.

- Use case studies to demonstrate realistic outcomes.

4.2 Phased Implementation

- Start with small, well-defined pilot projects before scaling AI across the organization.

- Example: Begin with automating simple customer support queries before deploying an advanced chatbot.

---

5. Optimizing Costs and Resources

5.1 Leveraging Cloud Computing

- Use cloud platforms like AWS, Google Cloud, or Azure to access scalable AI resources without significant upfront costs.

5.2 Open-Source Tools

- Adopt open-source frameworks like TensorFlow, PyTorch, and Scikit-learn to reduce software expenses.

5.3 Collaboration and Grants

- Partner with research institutions or apply for government grants to fund AI initiatives.

---

6. Ensuring Ethical AI

6.1 Bias Audits

- Regularly audit datasets and models for biases using tools like IBM AI Fairness 360 or Google's What-If Tool.

6.2 Ethical Frameworks

- Develop an internal code of ethics for AI projects, emphasizing fairness, accountability, and transparency.

6.3 Transparency and Explainability

- Use explainable AI (XAI) techniques to make model decisions interpretable to users.

- Example: Implement SHAP (Shapley Additive Explanations) to explain predictions in decision-making systems.

Adapting to Rapidly Changing Technologies

The field of AI evolves at an unprecedented pace, with new tools, techniques, and frameworks emerging regularly. Staying competitive requires adaptability and a commitment to continuous learning.

---

1. Embracing Continuous Learning

1.1 Staying Updated

- Follow reputable AI blogs, journals, and conferences like NeurIPS, CVPR, and AAAI to keep abreast of the latest advancements.

1.2 Encouraging Experimentation

- Allocate resources for experimentation with emerging technologies like GPT models, federated learning, or quantum AI.

---

2. Building Resilient Infrastructure

2.1 Modular Design

- Build modular AI systems that can be easily upgraded or replaced as new technologies emerge.

2.2 Cloud-Native Architecture

- Leverage cloud-native principles to ensure scalability and flexibility in deploying AI solutions.

---

3. Collaborating and Partnering

3.1 Industry Partnerships

- Partner with tech companies or startups to access cutting-edge AI tools and expertise.

3.2 Open Innovation

- Participate in open-source projects to contribute to and benefit from collective advancements in AI.

4. Planning for Long-Term Impact

4.1 Strategic Roadmaps

- Develop a roadmap that aligns AI adoption with organizational goals and anticipated technological trends.

4.2 Lifelong Learning Ecosystems

- Create an ecosystem where employees can continuously learn and adapt to new AI tools and methodologies.

Implementing AI is a complex yet rewarding journey fraught with technical, organizational, and ethical challenges. By understanding common roadblocks—such as data quality issues, skill shortages, and system integration difficulties—and adopting targeted strategies, organizations can significantly improve their chances of success. Adapting to rapidly evolving AI technologies requires continuous learning, collaboration, and strategic planning. With these approaches, businesses can unlock AI's transformative potential and position themselves at the forefront of innovation.

Chapter 20: Hands-On Projects for Beginners and Beyond

One of the most effective ways to learn machine learning (ML) and artificial intelligence (AI) is by engaging in hands-on projects. Practical experience not only reinforces theoretical knowledge but also introduces you to real-world challenges such as data preprocessing, feature engineering, and model evaluation. This chapter presents three comprehensive projects designed for learners at different levels of expertise: predicting house prices using regression for beginners, building a chatbot with natural language processing (NLP) for intermediates, and training a convolutional neural network (CNN) for image classification for advanced learners.

Beginner Project: Predicting House Prices Using Regression

Objective

This project involves building a regression model to predict house prices based on various features such as square footage, number of bedrooms, and location. It introduces fundamental ML concepts like data preprocessing, linear regression, and model evaluation.

Step 1: Dataset Preparation

Dataset

Use a publicly available dataset such as the **Boston Housing Dataset** or **Kaggle's House Prices: Advanced Regression Techniques Dataset**. These datasets contain features like:

- **LotArea**: Lot size in square feet.

- **YearBuilt**: Year the house was built.

- **GrLivArea**: Above-ground living area in square feet.

- **SalePrice**: The target variable (price of the house).

Load the Data

python

```
import pandas as pd

# Load the dataset
data = pd.read_csv("house_prices.csv")
print(data.head())
```

Step 2: Data Preprocessing

1. **Handle Missing Values**

   o Fill missing values with the median for numerical columns or the mode for categorical columns.

python

```
data.fillna(data.median(), inplace=True)
```

2. **Feature Selection**

   o Select relevant features for the model, such as GrLivArea, YearBuilt, and LotArea.

3. **Encode Categorical Variables**

   ○ Convert categorical features (e.g., Neighborhood) into numerical values using one-hot encoding.

python

```
data = pd.get_dummies(data, columns=["Neighborhood"], drop_first=True)
```

4. **Normalize Numerical Features**

   ○ Scale features to a similar range for better model performance.

python

```
from sklearn.preprocessing import StandardScaler
scaler = StandardScaler()
data[['GrLivArea', 'YearBuilt', 'LotArea']] = scaler.fit_transform(data[['GrLivArea', 'YearBuilt', 'LotArea']])
```

Step 3: Model Building

1. **Split the Data**

   o Divide the dataset into training and testing sets.

python

```python
from sklearn.model_selection import train_test_split

X = data.drop("SalePrice", axis=1)

y = data["SalePrice"]

X_train, X_test, y_train, y_test = train_test_split(X, y, test_size=0.2, random_state=42)
```

2. **Train a Linear Regression Model**

python

```python
from sklearn.linear_model import LinearRegression

model = LinearRegression()

model.fit(X_train, y_train)
```

Step 4: Model Evaluation

1. **Predict on Test Data**

python

```
y_pred = model.predict(X_test)
```

2. **Evaluate Performance**

  o Use metrics like Mean Squared Error (MSE) and R-squared ($R2R^2R2$) to assess the model.

python

```
from sklearn.metrics import mean_squared_error, r2_score

mse = mean_squared_error(y_test, y_pred)

r2 = r2_score(y_test, y_pred)

print(f"MSE: {mse}, R2: {r2}")
```

Outcome

You've built a basic regression model to predict house prices. This project introduces essential ML concepts and prepares you for more complex tasks.

Intermediate Project: Building a Chatbot with NLP

Objective

Create a chatbot capable of answering user queries using Natural Language Processing (NLP). This project involves preprocessing text data, training a conversational model, and deploying it as an interactive application.

Step 1: Define the Scope

Functionality

- The chatbot will answer FAQs using predefined responses and learn from user queries over time.

Dataset

- Use an FAQ dataset or create one with sample questions and answers related to a specific domain, such as customer support.

Step 2: Data Preprocessing

1. **Tokenization**

   o Split sentences into words.

python

```
from nltk.tokenize import word_tokenize

data['tokenized'] =
data['question'].apply(word_tokenize)
```

2. **Stopword Removal**

   o Remove common words like "is,"
   "and," and "the" that do not add
   meaningful context.

python

```
from nltk.corpus import stopwords

stop_words = set(stopwords.words('english'))

data['filtered'] = data['tokenized'].apply(lambda x:
[word for word in x if word not in stop_words])
```

3. **Vectorization**

   o Convert text into numerical
   representations using techniques like
   TF-IDF or word embeddings.

python

```
from sklearn.feature_extraction.text import TfidfVectorizer

vectorizer = TfidfVectorizer()

X = vectorizer.fit_transform(data['question'])
```

Step 3: Build the Chatbot Model

1. **Train a Classifier**

   o Use a classifier like Naive Bayes or Logistic Regression to map user questions to predefined responses.

python

```
from sklearn.naive_bayes import MultinomialNB

model = MultinomialNB()

model.fit(X, data['response'])
```

2. **Predict Responses**

   o For new user inputs, tokenize, vectorize, and pass them to the model for prediction.

python

```python
user_input = "How can I reset my password?"

user_vector = vectorizer.transform([user_input])

response = model.predict(user_vector)

print(response)
```

Step 4: Deploy the Chatbot

1. **Interactive Interface**

    o Use a library like Flask to deploy the chatbot as a web application.

python

```python
from flask import Flask, request, jsonify

app = Flask(__name__)


@app.route('/chat', methods=['POST'])
def chat():
    user_input = request.json['message']
    user_vector = vectorizer.transform([user_input])
    response = model.predict(user_vector)
```

```
return jsonify({'response': response[0]})
```

2. **Run the Application**

bash

```
python app.py
```

Outcome

You've built a functional chatbot, reinforcing your NLP skills and introducing you to deployment concepts.

Advanced Project: Training a CNN for Image Classification

Objective

Build a convolutional neural network (CNN) to classify images into predefined categories. This project involves advanced concepts like deep learning, data augmentation, and GPU acceleration.

Step 1: Dataset Preparation

Dataset

Use a dataset like **CIFAR-10** (images of 10 object categories) or **MNIST** (handwritten digits).

Load the Dataset

python

```
from tensorflow.keras.datasets import cifar10

(X_train, y_train), (X_test, y_test) = cifar10.load_data()
```

Step 2: Data Preprocessing

1. **Normalize Pixel Values**

    o   Scale pixel values to a range of [0, 1] for faster convergence.

python

```
X_train = X_train / 255.0

X_test = X_test / 255.0
```

2. **One-Hot Encode Labels**

o   Convert categorical labels into one-hot encoded vectors.

python

```
from tensorflow.keras.utils import to_categorical
y_train = to_categorical(y_train, 10)
y_test = to_categorical(y_test, 10)
```

Step 3: Build the CNN Model

1. Define the Model Architecture

python

```
from tensorflow.keras.models import Sequential
from tensorflow.keras.layers import Conv2D, MaxPooling2D, Flatten, Dense, Dropout

model = Sequential([
    Conv2D(32, (3, 3), activation='relu', input_shape=(32, 32, 3)),
    MaxPooling2D((2, 2)),
    Conv2D(64, (3, 3), activation='relu'),
```

```
MaxPooling2D((2, 2)),

Flatten(),

Dense(128, activation='relu'),

Dropout(0.5),

Dense(10, activation='softmax')
```

```
])
```

2. **Compile the Model**

python

```
model.compile(optimizer='adam',
loss='categorical_crossentropy',
metrics=['accuracy'])
```

3. **Train the Model**

python

```
model.fit(X_train, y_train, epochs=10,
batch_size=32, validation_data=(X_test, y_test))
```

Step 4: Evaluate the Model

1. Test Accuracy

python

```python
test_loss, test_acc = model.evaluate(X_test, y_test)
print(f"Test Accuracy: {test_acc}")
```

2. Save the Model

python

```python
model.save("cnn_image_classifier.h5")
```

Step 5: Data Augmentation (Optional)

Use data augmentation to artificially expand the training dataset.

python

```python
from tensorflow.keras.preprocessing.image import ImageDataGenerator

datagen = ImageDataGenerator(rotation_range=15, horizontal_flip=True)

datagen.fit(X_train)
```

Outcome

You've trained a CNN to classify images, gaining hands-on experience with deep learning and advanced ML workflows.

Hands-on projects are essential for mastering AI and ML. By working on predicting house prices, building a chatbot, and training a CNN, you develop a wide range of skills—from regression and NLP to deep learning. These projects provide a solid foundation for tackling real-world problems and preparing for more advanced AI applications.

Chapter 21: Future Directions and Opportunities in AI

Artificial Intelligence (AI) has already transformed industries and everyday life, but its potential for the future remains boundless. As the field matures, new technologies, methodologies, and opportunities continue to emerge, pushing the boundaries of what AI can achieve. From leveraging quantum computing to advancing explainable and generative AI, the next decade promises to revolutionize how we understand and deploy intelligent systems. In this chapter, we explore the role of quantum computing in AI, delve into emerging fields such as explainable and generative AI, and highlight career paths and the importance of continuous learning in this dynamic field.

The Role of Quantum Computing in AI

Quantum computing, a cutting-edge paradigm in computational science, has the potential to redefine AI by addressing its most significant limitations—processing speed and scalability. While classical computers rely on binary logic, quantum computers leverage quantum bits (qubits) that can exist in multiple states simultaneously, enabling unprecedented computational power.

1. How Quantum Computing Enhances AI

1.1 Speeding Up Computations

Many AI tasks, such as training deep neural networks, are computationally intensive and time-consuming. Quantum computing can process complex calculations much faster than classical systems.

- **Example**: Training a deep learning model that takes weeks on classical GPUs might be completed in hours using a quantum computer.

1.2 Solving Optimization Problems

AI often involves solving optimization problems, such as finding the best weights for a neural network. Quantum computing's ability to explore multiple solutions simultaneously makes it ideal for these tasks.

- **Example**: Quantum algorithms like the Quantum Approximate Optimization

Algorithm (QAOA) can solve combinatorial optimization problems efficiently.

1.3 Enhancing Machine Learning Algorithms

Quantum algorithms can improve existing machine learning models by enabling faster linear algebra operations, such as matrix multiplication and inversion, which are fundamental to AI.

- **Example**: Quantum-enhanced Support Vector Machines (QSVMs) can classify data more efficiently than their classical counterparts.

---

2. Challenges in Quantum AI

2.1 Hardware Limitations

Quantum computers are still in their infancy, with limited qubits and error rates that affect reliability.

2.2 Accessibility

Quantum computing resources are expensive and primarily available through research institutions or tech giants like IBM, Google, and Microsoft.

2.3 Algorithm Development

Quantum-specific algorithms are still being developed, and adapting classical AI methods for quantum systems requires specialized knowledge.

3. Future Opportunities in Quantum AI

3.1 Drug Discovery

Quantum-powered AI could accelerate the identification of molecular compounds for diseases by simulating complex chemical interactions.

3.2 Climate Modeling

AI combined with quantum computing could create accurate climate models, enabling better predictions and solutions for environmental challenges.

3.3 Financial Optimization

Quantum AI can revolutionize financial markets by optimizing portfolios and improving risk analysis models.

Emerging Fields: Explainable AI and Generative AI

As AI systems grow in complexity, two emerging fields—Explainable AI (XAI) and Generative AI—are gaining prominence for their potential to enhance understanding, usability, and creativity in AI applications.

1. Explainable AI (XAI)

1.1 Why Explainability Matters

AI systems often function as "black boxes," providing outputs without explaining how decisions were made. Explainable AI aims to make these processes transparent, enabling users to trust and understand AI decisions.

- **Example**: In healthcare, an XAI system diagnosing a disease should explain its reasoning (e.g., identifying specific symptoms or patterns in medical imaging).

1.2 Key Techniques in XAI

1. **Model-Specific Methods**

   o Built-in techniques like attention mechanisms in transformers to highlight relevant features.

2. **Post-Hoc Analysis**

   o Tools like SHAP (Shapley Additive Explanations) and LIME (Local Interpretable Model-Agnostic Explanations) explain predictions of pre-trained models.

3. **Visualization Tools**

- o Heatmaps or feature importance charts show how input features influence predictions.

1.3 Applications of XAI

- **Healthcare**: Interpreting diagnoses to support doctors.

- **Finance**: Explaining credit scoring decisions.

- **Autonomous Vehicles**: Clarifying navigation decisions for safety audits.

Challenges in XAI

- Balancing explainability with model performance.

- Ensuring explanations are meaningful to non-technical stakeholders.

2. Generative AI

2.1 What is Generative AI?

Generative AI creates new content—text, images, music, or code—by learning patterns from existing data. Models like Generative Adversarial Networks (GANs) and transformers (e.g., GPT, DALL·E) power this field.

- **Example**: GPT-4 can generate human-like text, while DALL·E creates realistic images based on textual descriptions.

2.2 Applications of Generative AI

1. **Creative Industries**

   o Generating artwork, music, and scripts.

   o Example: Adobe's generative AI tools for graphic design.

2. **Healthcare**

   o Designing synthetic medical data for research.

   o Example: Generating patient datasets for rare diseases to improve model training.

3. **Entertainment**

   o Creating video game assets, dialogue, and characters dynamically.

4. **Product Design**

   o Generating prototypes for industrial designs.

2.3 Ethical Considerations

- **Deepfakes**: Misuse of generative AI for creating fake content poses security and privacy risks.

- **Copyright Issues**: Ensuring that generative models respect intellectual property rights.

Future Trends in Generative AI

- Real-time generation for augmented and virtual reality (AR/VR).

- Advanced multimodal models combining text, image, and video generation.

Career Paths and Continuous Learning in AI

AI's rapid evolution offers numerous career opportunities for aspiring professionals. However, staying relevant in this dynamic field requires lifelong learning and adaptability.

---

1. Career Paths in AI

1.1 Data Scientist

- **Role**: Analyze data, build ML models, and derive insights to solve business problems.

- **Skills**: Data analysis, Python, R, SQL, and visualization tools like Tableau.

1.2 Machine Learning Engineer

- **Role**: Design, build, and deploy ML models into production systems.

- **Skills**: TensorFlow, PyTorch, distributed systems, and cloud platforms like AWS or Azure.

1.3 AI Researcher

- **Role**: Develop new AI algorithms and push the boundaries of AI capabilities.

- **Skills**: Mathematics, algorithm development, and academic writing.

1.4 AI Product Manager

- **Role**: Oversee AI projects, bridge the gap between technical teams and stakeholders, and align AI solutions with business goals.

- **Skills**: Project management, business acumen, and a foundational understanding of AI.

1.5 AI Ethicist

- **Role**: Ensure AI systems align with ethical principles and societal values.

- **Skills**: Policy-making, ethics, and an understanding of AI technologies.

---

2. Building a Career in AI

2.1 Start with the Basics

- Learn programming languages like Python and foundational ML libraries (Scikit-learn, NumPy, Pandas).

2.2 Gain Hands-On Experience

- Work on projects like image classification, chatbot creation, or predictive analytics.

2.3 Stay Updated

- Follow AI research papers, blogs, and conferences (e.g., NeurIPS, ICML).

2.4 Specialize

- Focus on niche areas like NLP, computer vision, or reinforcement learning to stand out in the job market.

---

3. Continuous Learning in AI

3.1 Online Learning Platforms

- **Coursera and edX**: Offer AI courses from top universities.

- **Kaggle**: Provides datasets and competitions to hone ML skills.

- **YouTube Channels**: Follow educators like Andrew Ng and Yannic Kilcher for insights.

3.2 Certifications

- **Google AI Certification**: Validates skills in TensorFlow and ML pipelines.

- **AWS Machine Learning Specialty**: Focuses on deploying ML in cloud environments.

3.3 Building a Portfolio

- Showcase projects on GitHub or Kaggle to demonstrate practical expertise.

3.4 Networking

- Join AI-focused meetups, hackathons, and LinkedIn groups to connect with peers and industry leaders.

The future of AI is brimming with possibilities, from the transformative potential of quantum computing to the creative innovations enabled by generative AI. As the field expands, explainable AI will ensure transparency and trust, while career paths in AI will continue to diversify, catering to a wide range of interests and expertise. Embracing continuous learning and staying adaptable are vital for those seeking to thrive in this ever-changing landscape. By understanding and engaging with these emerging directions and opportunities, professionals and organizations can position themselves at the forefront of AI's next wave of innovation.

Conclusion

Artificial Intelligence (AI) is a transformative force that is reshaping industries, enhancing human capabilities, and addressing some of the world's most pressing challenges. Throughout this book, we have explored the breadth and depth of AI, from its fundamental concepts and methodologies to its real-world applications and future potential. This conclusion serves as a synthesis of the key insights covered, emphasizing the opportunities, challenges, and responsibilities that come with leveraging AI in the modern world.

A Journey Through AI: Key Takeaways

1. Foundations of AI and Machine Learning

At its core, AI is about creating systems that can mimic human intelligence, learn from data, and adapt to new challenges. Machine learning (ML), a subset of AI, provides the tools and algorithms that make this possible. From supervised learning to unsupervised learning and reinforcement learning, understanding these paradigms equips us to tackle diverse problems across domains.

What We Learned

- **Supervised Learning**: Models like linear regression and decision trees are ideal for tasks with labeled data, such as predicting house prices or diagnosing diseases.

- **Unsupervised Learning**: Clustering techniques like K-means help uncover hidden patterns in data, such as customer segmentation.

- **Reinforcement Learning**: By learning through trial and error, RL algorithms enable applications such as autonomous vehicles and game-playing AI.

---

2. The Power of Data

Data is the lifeblood of AI. High-quality, well-preprocessed data ensures the reliability and accuracy of ML models. From understanding data types to preprocessing techniques and feature engineering, we've highlighted the importance of preparing data as a critical step in the AI pipeline.

Takeaway

Investing in robust data collection, cleaning, and transformation processes is essential for building effective AI systems. Furthermore, addressing issues such as bias, incompleteness, and data silos ensures fairness and inclusivity in AI outcomes.

---

3. The Role of Advanced Techniques

Deep learning and neural networks have revolutionized the AI landscape by enabling breakthroughs in fields like natural language processing (NLP) and computer vision. Technologies such as convolutional neural networks (CNNs) for image recognition and transformers for language tasks showcase AI's potential to tackle complex, unstructured data.

Key Insights

- Neural networks are the backbone of modern AI systems, enabling applications like facial recognition, real-time language translation, and autonomous systems.

- Feature engineering remains a critical skill, as even the most sophisticated models depend on well-crafted input features.

---

4. Real-World Applications

AI's influence spans industries and geographies, solving practical problems and unlocking new opportunities. From healthcare to finance, education, and beyond, the real-world applications of AI demonstrate its transformative power.

Examples of Impact

- **Healthcare**: Early detection of diseases, personalized medicine, and efficient drug discovery.

- **Finance**: Fraud detection, algorithmic trading, and personalized financial planning.

- **Education**: Adaptive learning platforms that personalize content for students based on their strengths and weaknesses.

---

5. The Need for Ethical and Responsible AI

While the benefits of AI are immense, the risks and challenges it poses cannot be ignored. Ethical considerations—such as addressing bias, ensuring transparency, and protecting privacy—are integral to building trust in AI systems. The rise of explainable AI (XAI) reflects the demand for greater accountability in decision-making systems.

Key Lessons

- Ethical frameworks should guide the development and deployment of AI to ensure fairness, inclusivity, and social good.

- Organizations must proactively address biases in datasets and algorithms to prevent perpetuating inequalities.

The Challenges and Opportunities Ahead

The AI landscape is dynamic, with rapid advancements and evolving challenges. Scaling AI models, integrating them into legacy systems, and adapting to cutting-edge technologies like quantum computing require agility, expertise, and foresight.

1. Overcoming Challenges

The road to effective AI implementation is not without obstacles. Challenges such as data silos, talent shortages, and unrealistic expectations must be addressed to unlock AI's full potential.

Strategies for Success

- **Collaboration**: Foster cross-disciplinary teams that combine domain expertise, technical skills, and business acumen.

- **Continuous Learning**: Stay updated on the latest advancements in AI tools, techniques, and methodologies.

- **Infrastructure**: Invest in scalable, cloud-based solutions to support AI pipelines and workflows.

2. Exploring New Frontiers

Emerging fields like generative AI and quantum computing promise to redefine what's possible with AI. Generative AI is already creating content, designs, and prototypes, while quantum computing holds the potential to solve problems that are currently intractable for classical systems.

Opportunities to Watch

- **Generative AI**: Advancements in models like GPT and DALL·E are enabling AI to generate human-like text, images, and even music.

- **Quantum AI**: With its unparalleled computational power, quantum computing could revolutionize fields like cryptography, logistics, and drug discovery.

AI as a Catalyst for Change

AI is not just a technology; it is a catalyst for change. Its ability to enhance human creativity, automate repetitive tasks, and solve complex problems positions it as a driving force for innovation and societal progress.

1. AI for Social Good

AI is increasingly being used to address global challenges, from climate change to healthcare accessibility. Examples include:

- **Disaster Prediction**: AI models forecast natural disasters, enabling timely responses.

- **Wildlife Conservation**: AI-powered drones monitor endangered species and combat poaching.

- **Global Health**: AI identifies disease outbreaks and accelerates vaccine development.

2. AI and the Workforce

AI's role in the workforce is evolving. While automation may replace certain jobs, it also creates new opportunities and augments human capabilities. Upskilling and reskilling initiatives will be critical for navigating this transition.

3. A Vision for the Future

The future of AI is one of collaboration—where humans and machines work together to achieve more than either could alone. This symbiotic relationship will empower individuals, organizations, and societies to solve problems at unprecedented scales.

A Call to Action

For businesses, researchers, and learners alike, AI represents both a responsibility and an opportunity. By investing in education, fostering innovation, and adhering to ethical principles, we can harness AI's transformative potential responsibly and equitably.

For Learners

Start small, experiment often, and continuously build your skills. From predicting house prices to training neural networks, hands-on projects are the gateway to mastering AI.

For Businesses

Adopt a long-term, strategic approach to AI. Focus on creating value for customers, empowering employees, and addressing societal challenges.

For Researchers

Continue pushing the boundaries of what AI can achieve while prioritizing ethical considerations and equitable access to its benefits.

Conclusion: Embracing the Possibilities of AI

Artificial Intelligence is more than just a tool—it is a transformative technology that is reshaping how we live, work, and interact with the world. While the path to widespread AI adoption is fraught with challenges, the opportunities it offers are unparalleled. By approaching AI with curiosity, responsibility, and a commitment to learning, we can create a future where its benefits are shared by all.

The journey with AI has just begun, and its potential is as vast as our collective imagination.

www.ingramcontent.com/pod-product-compliance
Lightning Source LLC
LaVergne TN
LVHW022335060326
832902LV00022B/4058